The Mind of Christ

D1100920

The Mind of Christ

David Scott

continuum

Continuum
The Tower Building
11 York Road
London SE1 7NX

80 Maiden Lane
Suite 704
New York
NY 10038

www.continuumbooks.com

First published 2007

British Library Cataloguing-in-Publication Data
A catalogue record for this book is available from the British Library.

ISBN 0-8264-9074-3

Typeset by TechBooks, New Delhi, India
Printed and bound by Ashford Colour Press Ltd., Gosport, Hants.

Contents

Introduction

'It is not literally the face of Jesus that we have to seek; the picturing imagination will not greatly aid us. We seek his heavenly mind. We must be bold, therefore, to conceive what it is like to be minded as he is minded . . . we must be Christ in his thought, as far as we are able.' *Austin Farrer*[1]

The college sermon at theological college was always a crucial moment for those of us who were soon to go out from the womb of student days to the coal-face of parish life. For the sermon you could preach on anything you wanted and choose your own text, and it was preached before the whole college. The choice was vertiginous, but generally people spoke from their heart the one thing that had become most important to them in the course of their life and training. One threw all his notes in the air and stepped down; one chose the compass points of Donne's famous poem about lovers. Roly Bain, I read recently in his autobiography, preached on clowning. Looking back, the sermon was probably a symbol of what the future held in the way of life choices and style of ministry.

I preached in a very discursive way about trying to put on the mind of Christ. I hope it wasn't entirely delusions of grandeur but it was a time when feelings and thoughts, the heart and the head, had met in some sort of creative tension, and that phrase of Paul's, 'put on the mind of Christ' pointed to a life's work. Through childhood and school, faith had been very much about sensing the presence of God and responses to that from the heart. The rollercoaster emotional life was uppermost through those years, responding to church services, the language of worship, the glories of the landscape, and the secrets of poetry written and read. It was all very much an affair of the heart.

Then came the challenge of theology. Feeling sure that in the end I would like to be ordained, theology seemed to be the most suitable subject to study at university and slipping into a church college under the disguise of an English literature student, I then changed courses and took on the challenge of academic theology. It was a bracing and in some ways a romantic choice. I had read about Abelard and the medieval schools and been deeply influenced by the poetry of John Donne. What I hadn't bargained for was the complexity of Greek and Hebrew verbs and the closeness we had to achieve in relation to the text of scripture. Most important of all was that it provided the stimulus and challenge to discuss how we can know anything about Jesus, let alone unlock the sanctuary of his mind. It was at this time that the clash between what I felt and what I thought began to pitch its battle.

Five years later I climbed the steps of the pulpit in that incomparable Oxfordshire church, from which I had heard Archbishop Ramsey preach the Three Hours only a few months before. The chosen text was a last-minute addition, 'and Jesus went off into the hills by himself', not exactly because that was going to be the subject of the sermon, but because that sort of escape route was my preferred option at that particular time. I wanted to take Jesus and his love of solitude into the pulpit with me. I felt sure that it was in such times of solitude that Jesus' mind would have been most creatively nurtured and the substance of the sermon was to do with how we might come closer to the mystery of that mind.

In the 35 years of ministry since then, the theme of how we 'put on the mind of Christ' still hovers over me. What that phrase, with its concentration on 'mind', does not immediately evoke is the way in which the rattle-bag of feelings about things, the heartaches, the heart searchings, the lifting up of the heart have coalesced and been informed by the sharper, tougher attitudes of mind. We shall see in the case of Jesus that those two concepts, heart and mind, become one orientation, attitude and spring for action. They also provide one unmoveable pointer for us to a destination we trust in, as we set out to know Christ, and are known by him, and so to enter into a creative relationship with the very centre of our faith.

Picking up the pen on a Saturday night to finalize the following day's sermon, the text has focused a kaleidoscope of different thoughts and feelings. We ask, 'what is it about this text, this word, this action, this parable that reveals one layer more for me about what God is trying to show through Jesus?'

I've always been a great devourer of ecclesiastical biography. I've wanted to know how people have got where they are, what major influences have been pressing upon them, and where they have experienced what they have experienced – the terrain, the landscape, the weather – both spiritual and physical. Mostly they have been modern biographies, in which the account seems to be quite straightforward. There has been for the last 200 years only one way of writing about a person's life: you begin at the beginning, go through the life until death, and then stop. The New Testament, at least the gospels, have a similar narrative thrust with Jesus' life, but there are big gaps in what we now consider to be crucial formative periods in a person's life, such as the period of childhood. It is these differences in biographical writing which make a straightforward attempt to copy Jesus, to 'put on the mind of Christ', a complex one and one, because of its complexity, of continuing fascination.

My journey through ministry between the late sixties and the beginning of the third millennium has had to encompass the reality of modern, scientific procedures in every sphere of life. This includes most importantly a searching critique of the literary evidence for the life of Christ and also of the mind that seeks to discover the mind of another. On one level nothing seems stable, and nothing can be said that cannot be contradicted about life, Jesus, God, anything. I suppose that's why we hammer in markers forged in existentialism, just to say that what we feel about something has a certain validity about it, regardless almost of anything else. It may not be universally true, but if it's true for me then it has at least the quality of personal truth, integrity, and meaning. In that personal reality, which is such a common experience in religious belief, the experience of things stopping, being fixed, being as we say, true, might well be as true as we can get.

I suppose it's as a result of feeling that we are never intellectually going to 'know' all the answers about God, that something else has to fill that void, or better still, that makes sense of the void. Prayer, the intimate relationship with God, redefines the nature of truth. What is true about God is what we discover when we spend time with God and similarly with Christ it is as we commit ourselves to him that we begin to redefine what is true about ourselves and about love. We begin to come at the mind of Christ like our first attempts at swimming, with trust that what is beneath us will hold us. This sheer rock face of theology with few obvious handholds and the huge sense of danger at being wrong is the way it often feels as soon as we come off our knees and leave the room. Yet on our knees, in private, with the door shut and an open heart everything seems less vulnerable to criticism and the judgement of the world at large. 'I am here. God is there. So let us rest'. The mind and the heart coalesce when all the books are put away and the soul is touched by love and the sound of it rings on the air.

Behind all this lies both the command to 'put on the Lord Jesus Christ' (Rom. 13.14) and the fascination for what that might mean in practice. Even if we can't reach perfection, we can get closer, and that in itself is worth it. To sail as close to the original meaning of the text as we can is obviously not something we 'must' do or 'have to do' to gain salvation. It is something that has arisen for me partly through fascination and partly through the grim deter-mination to master something that at first seemed so complex and confusing. However, in the end, I think it was the need to be as close as I could get in whatever way I could to someone whose life has captivated so many in this world and the idea of being a dis-ciple, which was attractive. That demanded and still demands the utmost rigour in intelligent thought and sensitivity to image, word and history. Above all it involves an attention to the relationship between knowledge and faith, not as opposites, but as allies. Blind faith is fine if that, shall we say, is what God has given us. Yet the adventure of using one's own mind to bring us alongside the mind of someone who has had such a crucial effect on our understand-ing of what a life can be, is also, I find, irresistible. The command has become compelling and the fascination enters in when we begin to live with the consequences of our calling. We may wander a long way from the original nature of our commitment but the echo of the voice that called us still calls us back to the root and ground of our faith in Jesus Christ.

Chapter 1

'But who do you say I am?'

Naming Christ

One of the first things we ask of anyone whom we want to know better is their name. A person's name tells us some basic and important information about them, but from the word go, that is not simple. We have several names, first names or Christian names, and a surname, which means a name in addition which is often a family name. To these fairly basic and universal names are added 'nick-names' meaning a lengthened name and now understood to be a familiar name indicating an aspect of the person's character or physique, like 'Titch' or 'Lofty'.

When we come to study Jesus we learn a great deal about him both by the names he was given and also by the names or titles he seemed to prefer to use for himself. Titles are usually conferred on a person by others, but it is also possible to let it be known that you prefer one title rather than another. 'How do you like to be addressed?' and 'What do you like to be called?' are questions often asked of the clergy, because people are never quite sure what all the possible names and titles indicate, 'Father', 'Vicar', 'Canon', 'Reverend'.

Jesus is a basic name, a first name. Traditionally it was the name that the Angel Gabriel proclaimed that Mary's child should be called (Lk. 1.31). It was a common Hebrew boy's name and signified 'Yahweh saves'. We read in English the transliteration of the Greek version of the Hebrew name. Since the name was common, one Jesus was distinguished from another by the appellation of the home town, and so we get *Jesus of Nazareth*. I think it is fair to say that we feel comfortable with the name 'Jesus'. In one way it is as familiar as Tom, Dick and Harry, but because of who Jesus was and what he did, it has come to have an additional resonance, or power.

The use of the name 'Jesus' became a means of performing miracles, because name and character were so intertwined. To say the name was to be in receipt of the power of the name. The disciples performed miracles and exorcisms 'in the name of Jesus', that is, by his power (Mk. 9.39f.; Acts 4.30) and regularly baptized in the name (Acts 2.38, 8.16) and Paul especially insists on its efficacy for our justification (1 Cor. 6.11) and the obligation of Christians to venerate it above all names (Phil. 2.7f.)

Yet there are a host of other titles associated with Jesus of Nazareth, each one representing a complex and subtle aspect of how others saw his character and explained his purpose. Such titles are 'Lord', 'Master' and 'Teacher', denoting the reverence in which he was held. 'You call me Teacher and Lord – and you are right for that is what I am. So if I, your Lord and Teacher, have washed your feet, you ought also to wash one another's feet' (Jn. 13.13–14). With the use of 'Lord' and 'Master' we are still working with titles which give dignity to others. Yet there are other titles that are more complex because they relate the human Jesus to the supernatural power of God, such as 'Son of God', or 'Messiah'. In this area, complex issues of interpretation arise, such as the claiming of titles that are not deserved, of assuming titles which are not appropriate, and of sorting out the cultural and religious associations that go with the titles which are beyond our easy reach of understanding. Having said that, they are also the most important and the most interesting because they lead us closer to the reality of Jesus' understanding of himself, and this comes to the heart of the exploration of this book. It is not just what *we* think about Jesus or what Jesus thinks about us, but what Jesus thought about himself, his self-consciousness, that is the thing that most interests me.

This detective work takes some grasping because there are many layers of meaning and interpretation. To put on the mind of Christ inevitably involves us in asking the question 'what mind' are we absorbing? If we want to see the world as Jesus saw it, with similar priorities, and to reflect just a fraction of his divinity, then every step into the world of his times, and sympathy with his intentions, will help us to put on his mind and see through his eyes.

For example, let us see what is going on in this passage from John 19, which describes a detail from the crucifixion of Jesus. Pilate, the Roman governor, is keen to have a notice nailed to the cross that reads 'Jesus of Nazareth, the King of the Jews'. The chief priest of the Jews was dissatisfied with Pilate's notice and insisted on a correction that would read, 'This man *said*, I am the King of the Jews.' The correction would then have laid the blame squarely on Jesus' shoulders, because he was claiming the kingship without any justification.

> So they took Jesus; and carrying the cross by himself he went out to what is called The Place of the Skull, which in Hebrew is Golgotha. There they crucified him, and with him two others, one on either side, with Jesus between them. Pilate also had an inscription written and put on the cross. It read, 'Jesus of Nazareth, the King of the Jews.' Many of the Jews read this inscription, because the place where Jesus was crucified was near the city; and it was written in Hebrew, in Latin, and in Greek. Then the chief priest of the Jews said to Pilate, 'Do not write, "The King of the Jews" but, "This man said, I am the King of the Jews."' Pilate answered, 'What I have written I have written.' (Jn. 19.16–22).

How amazing that even as Jesus was about to be crucified there was a wrangle over words. It is only in John's gospel that this particular detail is recorded, as with so many other precise and minute details of the life of Jesus. John's camera, if he had had one, would have been getting in close, sensitively picking up the detail that tells a larger story. But it is not just visual detail that John shows us, it is also and most particularly a matter of language and in this case languages plural. Three main languages were in the frame at the time of Jesus' crucifixion: Hebrew, Latin and Greek.

It is those languages that have given subtle variations of meaning to the whole gospel, starting with the names of Jesus.

'Then the chief priests of the Jews said to Pilate, "Do not write, 'The King of the Jews' but, 'This man said, I am the King of the Jews.'"' (Jn. 19.21) There is something absurd about an argument over what should be written on a cross. The chief priests of the Jews, pedantically we might think, want the inscription to carry the full innuendo of Jesus' claim to kingship. The scandal was in the claim, not just that people thought that he was the King of the Jews, but that Jesus himself had claimed the title that belonged only to God. What subtleties! Such a perception of self-consciousness! That John could have considered it important to record distinctions so subtle is remarkable. This zoom-lens penetration into motives was not always a major factor in the earliest gospel records, but in John's gospel it was: 'write "this man *said*, I am the King of the Jews"'. It is a wonderful though tragic subtlety to be demanded at a moment of agony, pain and confusion and it does seem a very 'modern' concern to get back to the motives, to get into the mind of a person. The excitement is almost archaeological, to pare back the layers. First there is the layer of the chief priest's claim, then the layer of why the evangelist John added the fact when no one else did, and then the layer of what the other gospels said of Jesus' claims to kingship. Finally there is the enigma at the heart of it all, which is the indication of what Jesus himself might have thought. That of course we shall never know for certain, but the attempt may enlighten us about Jesus' method and meaning.

The fact that Jesus had so many names attached to him in the course of the New Testament is some indication of the complexity of his status and his personality and a sign of the many ways in which people saw and understood him. A person's name is an important focus of power. To know someone's name was thought to be a way into their nature, their inner selves, and to say the name was to be dealing in a sort of power. When Moses came close to God on the mountain he asked God what his name was so that he could tell others, and God's reply was remarkable; he said 'I AM

WHO I AM', and further, 'Thus you shall say to the Israelites, "I AM has sent me to you"'(Ex. 3.14). That always seems something of an ultimate sort of name: 'my name, my nature is the source of existence itself. I am the very root and ground of being. "I am that I am"'. Peter too, the disciple of Jesus, had a similar conversation with Jesus about names. Jesus asks the disciples who people thought he was and the answers came back 'John the Baptist; and others (said), Elijah; and still others, one of the prophets. He asked them, "But who do *you* say I am?" Peter answered him, "You are the Messiah." And he sternly ordered them not to tell anyone about him' (Mk. 8.27–30). Then, if that was not cryptic enough, Jesus goes on to describe himself in terms of 'the Son of Man', shifting the emphasis from a title of power and glory, to one of representative humanity. It was also a title that, in Jewish minds, would have had a particular role in the events that ushered in the kingdom of God at the end of time, as for example in Mk. 14.62f.

> you will see the Son of Man
> seated at the right hand of the Power,
> and coming with the clouds of heaven.

The words 'But who do you say I am?' seem to come calling out of the night directly to the personal part of the disciple in me. I have to, want to, make some sort of a stab at saying what is the nature of this person who speaks to me, compels me, invites me on into the adventure of faith. What name has he offered me? *Jesus* is the simplest and most direct name to grasp. With that name he seems to offer his simplest self, a self stripped of power and prestige. Yet how often do I also want to cry the exalted 'My God'? In prayer, in the times of offering ourselves to God, his name, his nature will come to us, be shared with us, and we shall know him at a level deeper than names, labels, or words. We shall know him as presence and in a way that encourages us to know ourselves as loved and our identity absorbed in his.

In searching for his name, his nature, we discover that his nature is best known in his knowing and calling our name. Samuel is brought to the Temple in Jerusalem by his mother and left in the care of Eli the priest. In the night Samuel thinks that Eli is calling him and he gets up and goes to the priest and says to him 'Here I am. What do you want?' And Eli sends him back to bed, not having called him at all. Once or twice more this happens until Eli realizes that the child Samuel is being called by the Lord, called in the night by name to lead a life in which God's name will be honoured and praised through Samuel. In the New Testament the disciples are called by name and some are given new names. Simon is called Peter, the rock; the rock on which the church's foundations were to be built and in whom the Church was to have its first leader.

***

Names and titles abound. In some senses they remain clumsy approximations to deeper identities held in the mind of God, yet the name too takes on an identity, a patina of meaning, when we grow into our name and to a certain extent we become more and more who we are meant to be. A calling to discipleship by God is a profound experience and a real one, though often difficult to elaborate in greater detail. There is no doubt that it has a very personal element. People acknowledge that God seems to know them personally and they respond to being known, challenged and loved. Saul of Tarsus, persecutor of Christians, is stopped in his tracks on the Damascus Road and surrounded by a light from heaven. He falls to the ground and hears a voice saying to him '"Saul, Saul why do you persecute me?" He asked, "Who are you, Lord?" The reply came, "I am Jesus, whom you are persecuting."' (Acts 9.4–5). Saul heard a call from Jesus himself and this moved him to become the great interpreter of the purposes of Christ for the emerging Church.

In more humble and more chaotic and ill-defined circumstances I felt a call, but it came without a particular brief. There was no voice, no orders, no direction, and no name. So what was it about that call that held within it a compulsion to serve God and be in his service whatever happened? Let me put it like this. It was more a sense of being taken over by love, by being orientated towards God whose nature was love. It was also a sense of being alongside a power, a person, a will, that would hold me whatever I was, and wherever I went, and whatever I did. I thought this was being called, a being known. It was not something that I felt I had generated within myself. God had taken up my nature and from then on owned it and seemed to have taken it to himself for his own purposes. My easy task was to rejoice and obey and the difficult task was to be worthy of it.

In the mystical writings of Dionysius the Pseudo-Areopagite (*c*. 500) on *The Divine Names* there is a section on God as yearning and love. There the writer gets close to an understanding of God as both call and response. God seems to call out from within a person what is something essentially his own. What was placed within from the beginning of time, within the one who loves and yearns, finds its home again in the one who calls. So when God calls your name, his is the name that is being called:

> Why is it that theologians sometimes refer to God as Yearning and Love and sometimes the yearned-for and the Beloved? On the one hand God causes, produces, and generates what is being referred to, and, on the other hand, he is the thing itself. He is stirred by it and he stirs it. He is moved to it and he moves it. So they call him the beloved and the yearned-for since he is beautiful and good, and, again, they call him yearning and love because he is the power moving and lifting up all things to himself, for in the end what is he if not Beauty and Goodness, the One who of himself reveals himself, the good procession of his own transcendent unity?[2]

No wonder we feel a sense of the dance in reading and imagining this, as the call of God calls out to something within us which is God himself in embryo. 'He is yearning on the move, simple, self-moved, self-acting, pre-existent in the Good, flowing out from the Good onto all that is and returning once again to the Good. In this, divine yearning shows especially its unbeginning and unending nature travelling in an endless circle through the Good, from the Good, in the Good and to the Good, unerringly, turning, ever on the same centre, ever in the same direction, always proceeding, always remaining, always being restored to itself.'[3]

How strange that we have no writing from Jesus himself. If we have writings from his time and writings way before his time then it would have been quite possible to have writings from him, but it does not seem to have been so. He talked rather than wrote and others did the writing for him, Mark perhaps, and John the evangelist. They were the ones who listened and wrote it down and wrote it up. They were the ones who remembered what he had said and how he had said it. They were the ones remembering and remembering slightly differently, or remembering from their own perspective and in their own language and from their own tradition. We get Jesus just ever so slightly at one remove. We get Jesus through some other person's lens. In some cases, as in the gospels, it is only a whisker away from the voice itself. We can pick up tones of anger, anger particularly because it is rare, and of frustration. Jesus, as described in Mark's first chapter, is angry as he heals the leper. 'Moved to pity' is a contested alternative reading, but some consider that unlikely. John Austin Baker comments,

Concern, care and compassion are wonderful things, and they do a lot of good. They patch up our poor, battered world. But it is anger that changes it. It is when we feel anger, the deep anger of God himself, whether at abuse or cruelty or exploitation or injustice or any other evil toward God's creatures, that we actually do something. God knows there is enough in our world to feel angry about. When will our Church learn to be angry about things that matter?[4]

We catch the hints of Jesus' thinking and the earnestness of his mission, but it is largely filtered through the minds of the evangelists, and, to be in the presence of Jesus, we often have to imagine the layers of interpretation taken away. And these layers continued to be painted on in the stretch of history between then and now. We see Jesus and hear him at some distance, as we struggle with words to describe what he was like, words that fit the reality, and so we enter a world where words slip and slide.

But why be so pessimistic? It can be that as we write we get as close as we can. The miracle of writing can convey Jesus' essential being and in that sense the gospels are see-through, because they evoke faith. That is their miracle and their wonder. Through all the inadequacies of human language the miracle of the 'word' plays its part. It does not always give us perfect knowledge, but it does something much more important. It is a channel for the offering of ourselves to the one who demands not human wisdom, but faith. It is remarkable how the scriptures convey the love of God through very human words, and come to think of it, they are after all the only ones we have.

***

The barrier over the frustration of language was the dominant feeling of that part of the journey of my life which were specifically the training years. The gap between faith, the heart's larder of love, and the need to find some way of making sense of the words and documents that were attempting to convey the nature of that faith. The pressure to answer questions and be 'clever', to move from a simple faith to an intellectual faith in which all the ramifications of the text were taken into consideration, led to an interest in poetry. Poetry was a middle ground between faith and intellect. Both were important, but the chemistry between the two created a mental environment, which was attuned to the way the gospels seemed to want to work.

In the gospels there is certainly a strong emphasis on faith as the way into truth, but the very strangeness of the gospels demanded in addition to faith a curiosity about the stuff of practical life, the boats on the shore, the sycamore tree Zacchaeus shinned up, the coin with Caesar's head on it. It was when these two seeming opposites were brought together that the creative tension emerged in poetry, a language that would hold the world and 'the other' together.

The more I went on, the more a variety of responses to putting on the mind of Christ seemed to appear. It has taken me quite some time to find a mechanism to calm the shaken snow scene in which the identity of Christ has become in any sense clear. It has taken a long time to feel confident to lay aside all the information and the feelings, the mental processes and the domination of the 'I', to be at peace and settled with 'Thou'. And still it is hard to look straight into the sun of the divine nature and fix a gaze that settles the restless spirit and brings peace that transcends human knowledge.

Notes

1 Austin Farrer, *Said and Sung* (London: The Faith Press, 1960), p. 152.
2 *Pseudo-Dionysius: The Complete Works* (London: SPCK, 1987), p. 82.
3 Ibid., p. 82f.
4 John Austin Baker, *Unpublished Sermon* (Winchester: St Lawrence Church, 2005).

Chapter 2

By way of imitation

It was a Sunday in the summer term at school and the chaplain invited two or three of us to go with him in his Land Rover to collect the preacher for Evensong. The preacher happened to be a Franciscan friar from the Anglican Society of St Francis. I knew nothing of monks and friars other than what I was reading in Chaucer for 'A' level English. We jumped at any excuse to get out of school and so off we went the thirty or so miles from Solihull to Droitwich and then through the winding lanes to Shrawley. That was not the end yet, though. From the village, a rough track winds up a hill and on the top of the hill, looking one way to Abberley Hill and another way to Astley Church, is a stable block, which is all that's left of a grand house.

An Anglican monk called William Sirr inhabited this old stable block from 1918 to 1936. Fr William was a member of the Society of the Divine Compassion, but he felt called to try out a particular vocation to a more retired monastic life, hoping that others would join him. Many visited but few stayed. When after restoring the stables to be suitable for a monastic community and filling the place with a sense of prayer, he fell ill and had to leave, not knowing what would become of the monastery.

The Revd Sidney King came to visit him on the last morning before Fr William left Glasshampton for the last time, and he wrote this.

As the years went on and I saw the Monastery take its form – the cells for Monks all prepared and yet no Monks – I ceased to enquire if any fresh Postulants had come, feeling it must be painful for him to speak of it. On this last morning when I saw him on his bed his face lit up in welcome. I asked him if I might pray with him, I knelt at what was his last prayer in the Monastery. I commended him to God and besought God's peace upon him.

When I rose from my knees he said, looking me straight in the face, serene and untroubled, apropos of nothing said in the interview or in the prayers, *"We must not mind being a failure – Our Lord died on the Cross a failure."* Words I can never forget, nor the tone of his serene, quiet repose in the Will of God. I knew in that absolute surrender of his will to God, he had entered into the victorious mind of our Saviour on the Cross and knew the ineffable peace which only the Saints very near to God can know; and into which nothing can break nor destroy.[1]

In time the Society of St Francis took over the care of Glasshampton and since then it has flourished as a community house for the Society and a place where many people have visited for retreats. It was to this place that we came that summer's afternoon in 1965 to collect the preacher for the evening service.

Before the Land Rover had struggled up the final severe incline, the chaplain stopped the car and we all got out. He stopped just so we could hear the stillness. It was a sort of deep stillness I had never heard before. Life up till then had never consciously just stopped. School was busy and noisy and silence was always a command or a punishment. This was freedom and love. This was a bath of silence which began in just nothingness and then moved into distant birdsong; and even that didn't break the silence – it was part of it. I recall now, but didn't then, the lines of Edward Thomas, as his train stopped momentarily at the station of Adlestrop:

> The steam hissed. Someone cleared his throat.
> No one left and no one came
> On the bare platform. . . .
> And for that minute a blackbird sang

> Close by, and round him, mistier
> Farther and farther, all the birds
> Of Oxfordshire and Gloucestershire.[2]

This, however, was Worcestershire and we had stopped a Land Rover not a train, but the sense of peace and silence and the growing distance of silence were exactly the same. Just a few minutes was enough to initiate me into the wonderful mystery of quiet and ever since then I have been marking life out in similar healing moments.

Back into the Land Rover, we drove up the last half mile as the surface of the track got more and more pitted and bumpy until we arrived at the top of the hill and our destination. There were views all around for miles. The garden of the monastery was a riot of flowers, and the tea and cakes were a revelation. We met the preacher and I immediately liked him. He was not at all the usual muscular Christian that was then the popular choice for preaching. He wore a brown habit, a white rope for a belt, and no socks, just sandals. So, no tie, no shoes to clean, no shirt with a top button to do up. He was young, quietly spoken and I later learnt that he had been a nurse before he had entered the order. I began to wonder how he would get on with the critical congregation at a compulsory Evensong back at school.

After tea we were taken on a visit to look round the monastery, which included the refectory where monks eat, the library, the 'cells' where they slept and no doubt prayed. Then we saw the chapel, the centre of their life, where there was a life-size figure of the crucified Christ on the otherwise bare east wall. Oh, and the cat, and we heard the bell rung. But it was time to get back to the world that I had almost forgotten existed. The Franciscan brother had no luggage, only a book which fitted into the cavernous pocket of his 'habit'. I couldn't quite get over the difference between the feeling of that God-filled sanctuary and the world outside. I knew home-sickness from having to go back to school at the beginning of term and now I was home-sick for that sense of place where as T. S. Eliot put it, 'prayer had been valid'. 'Valid' is a good word. It means strong, powerful and effective. I could feel the prayer there. No wonder I have returned over the last forty years and each time 'known it for the first time'.

We got back to school and the hundred or so boys and staff and some parents were sitting waiting for the routine of Evensong to begin. It came to the time of the sermon and this humble friar climbed the steps into the pulpit. I don't know what anyone else thought, but I was transfixed. 'Of course', I said to myself, 'religion is as simple as this. You don't have to be clever and wear an academic hood, or be a headmaster. You just had to love God enough to give up all your own possessions and say, basically, 'Here I am Lord!'

In the pulpit, the friar told the story of his life and what it was like for him to live in the monastery and then he pulled out of his pocket a book and talked for a while about that. The book was *The Imitation of Christ* by Thomas à Kempis. From that evening I remember only the title; other than that there was in me an overwhelming desire to find that simplicity, and to learn more about the inspiration which lay behind that choice of life.

The imitation of Christ

The combination of this simple Franciscan and a spiritual classic brought out of a cavernous pocket takes some contemplating. Both person and book in their different ways were models of the life of Christ. The Franciscan friar I could see. He even looked like what we might think Christ looked like. There are many ways through to the central and pivotal person whose example we are pursuing. Thomas à Kempis in some numinous way has managed to capture the essence of Christ and communicate it in words.

To open a book and be confronted by words like 'humility', 'solitude', or even by the word 'God' at an early age, moved me into a strange and exciting world of new meaning. I found a copy of *The Imitation of Christ* in the local bookshop and had just that experience of discovering a completely new world of language.

What was 'imitation'? What was 'humility'? What was this new world going to ask of me? How was I going to begin imitating Christ? My copy of *The Imitation of Christ* after all these years still falls open at the page with the title, 'On the Love of Solitude and Silence'. Here were some more words that spoke of worlds I was only just on the very edge of, but was eager to enter into more fully.

I think it must have been Thomas à Kempis who first encouraged me not to be afraid of being alone, which was certainly an issue in early life. Everyone else seemed to be having such a good time and there was I sitting at home alone. I felt it was probably all right and I enjoyed reading, but to discover from à Kempis that solitude was a positive thing was an affirming revelation. Solitude was not sad but an immensely creative resource that paradoxically strengthened a love for others and not the reverse. Times of solitude strengthened a sense of belonging to the world, because the link was forged through a love of God who made the world and with the One who knew all things. This was the first of many paradoxes that were to follow on the discovery of trust in God. Solitude in the presence of God was a way of being open to and part of everyone. The love of God in its particularity opened up a love of God in all things for all people.

Thomas à Kempis, an Augustinian monk, was born in 1380 at Kempen, on the border between Germany and the Netherlands. His parents were poor and with his brother he was sent to school at Deventer to the School of the Brethren of the Common Life. A great monastic leader, Jan Ruysbroeck (1293–1381), who died just after Thomas à Kempis was born, was instrumental in the development of à Kempis' life. He retired with two other priests to a hermitage at Groenendaal, near Brussels, where others joined them. In 1350 the group became the community of Canons Regular with Ruysbroek as Prior until his death. Groenendaal became prominent in the religious movement later known as 'Devotio Moderna', in which Thomas à Kempis became involved. The movement laid great stress on the inner life of the individual and encouraged methodical meditation especially on the life and passion of ·Christ, and it was in this tradition that à Kempis was nurtured.

In 1399 Thomas entered the House of the Canons Regular, near Zwolle. It was also a monastic community that followed the rule of St Augustine, and it is to St Augustine's writings that Thomas looked for the greatest inspiration. His elder brother was the co-founder and Prior of the community, and in 1406 Thomas à Kempis became a professed member. There he lived out the bulk of his long life, writing, preaching and copying manuscripts, and was widely sought after as a spiritual director.

Thomas à Kempis wrote works of very different kinds, but it is *The Imitation* that is his classic work and is most pervaded by a devotional spirit. It is thought to have been completed in 1441. There are three sections to the work. The first is a series of 'Counsels on the Spiritual Life', of which the chapter 'On the Love of Solitude and Silence' is one. It was this section of *The Imitation* that seemed to tie in with my deepest sense of where God may be found. I think the influence of Wordsworth at the time, with his strong sense of binding together the springs of creativity and the solitude he experienced in the natural world, would have provided a connection for me. Solitude was not a strange or off-putting word. On the contrary it was silent music to my ears, as for Wordsworth it was 'in the bliss of solitude' in which he recollected the deep things of life. But I hadn't yet connected it with the religious part of myself and so *The Imitation of Christ* built that bridge.

> Choose a suitable time for recollection and frequently consider the loving-kindness of God. Do not read to satisfy curiosity or to pass the time, but study such things as move your heart to devotion . . . It is easier to keep silence altogether than not to talk more than we should. It is easier to remain quietly at home than to keep due watch over ourselves in public. Therefore, whoever is resolved to live an inward and spiritual life must, with Jesus, withdraw from the crowd.[3]
>
> In silence and in quietness the devout soul makes progress and learns the hidden mysteries of the Scriptures. There she finds floods of tears in which she may nightly wash and be

cleansed (Ps. 6.6). For the further she withdraws from all the tumult of the world, the nearer she draws to her Maker. For God with His holy angels will draw near to him who withdraws himself from his friends and acquaintances. It is better to live in obscurity and to seek the salvation of his soul, than to neglect this even to work miracles.[4]

Lift up your eyes to God on high (Ps. 121.1; Isa. 40.26), and beg forgiveness for your sin and neglectfulness. Leave empty matters to the empty-headed, and give your attention to those things that God commands you. Shut the door upon you (Matt. 6.6), and call upon Jesus the Beloved. Remain with him in your cell, for you will not find so great a peace anywhere else.[5]

In the chapter 'On Close Friendship with Jesus', à Kempis recalls the excitement with which Mary Magdalene rose 'at once from her place where she wept, when Martha said, "The Master is come, and is asking for you" ', (Jn. 11.28). 'O happy the hour' writes à Kempis 'when Jesus calls us from tears to joy of spirit.'[6]

The second section of the book is called 'On Inward Consolation' and is shaped as a conversation between Christ and the Disciple. Thomas uses this dramatic form to give an immediacy and a personal quality to what could otherwise be dry theology. I am always surprised at how the book manages to combine this strict, monastic sense of discipline, which must be so off-putting to many coming as it does from a strange Catholic world, with luminous gospel simplicity and straightforwardness. Certainly for me it was a new world and one which I might have felt cautious about, but I began to understand and feel deep within that the paradoxes of à Kempis, of giving up to take on Christ, to be quiet to hear the most beautiful of sounds, and to retreat from the crowd to be with Christ, were the most human things of all. It seemed to be what we were made for.

Blessed are the eyes that are closed to outward things, but are open to inward things. Blessed are those who enter deeply into inner things, and daily prepare themselves to receive the secrets of heaven. Blessed are those who strive to devote themselves wholly to God, and free themselves from all the entanglements of the world. Consider these things, O my soul, and shut fast the doors against the desires of the senses, that you may hear what the Lord your God speaks within you.

Your beloved says: 'I am your Salvation, your Peace, and your Life; keep close to me and you shall find peace'.[7]

One of the pitfalls that the *Imitation* could easily have fallen into in writing of the spiritual life, is the feeling that we can do it all ourselves, and any success is worthy of praise. However, à Kempis is passionate about humility, and we are left in no doubt that the grace of God alone saves us. Christ speaks: 'It is so hard for you who are dust and nothingness to subject yourself to man for God's sake, when I the Almighty and most high, who created all things from nothing, humbly subjected myself to man for your sake (Jn. 13.14). Direct your anger against yourself, and let no swelling pride remain in you.'[8]

Thomas à Kempis knew that it was the imitation of the crucified Jesus that would be the most challenging part of discipleship. Jesus went to the cross alone, his disciples having deserted him. Thomas writes about this in the chapter entitled, 'On the Few Lovers of the Cross of Jesus'. In a way, it's something we all know about in theory, but when it comes to facing real-life situations of suffering, or of witness to the truth of Christ, we are put to the test. Fine words are one thing, but by our deeds we shall be known. The worth of our prayer will come in the deed and this very much links up our more spiritual side with how we really feel about pain, suffering and death.

Jesus has many who love his Kingdom in Heaven, but few who bear his cross (Lk. 14:27). He has many who desire comfort, but few who desire suffering. He finds many to share his feast, but few his fasting. All desire to rejoice with him, but few are willing to suffer for his sake. Many follow Jesus to the Breaking of Bread, but few to the drinking of the cup of his Passion. Many admire his miracles, but few follow him in the humiliation of his Cross. Many love Jesus as long as no hardship touches them. Many praise and bless him, as long as they are receiving any comfort from him. But if Jesus withdraw himself, they fall to complaining and utter dejection.[9]

John Wesley was one of the great admirers of *The Imitation of Christ*. Is it possible that the inspiration for some of the words in the Methodist Covenant service came from *The Imitation*? 'Christ has many services to be done: some are easy, others are difficult; some bring honour, others bring reproach; some are suitable to our natural inclinations and temporal interests, others are contrary to both. In some we may please Christ and please ourselves, *in others we cannot please Christ except by denying ourselves*. Yet the power to do all these things is assuredly given us in Christ, who strengtheneth us. Therefore let us make the Covenant of God our own. Let us engage our heart to the Lord, and resolve in His strength never to go back.'[10]

Thomas à Kempis was an Augustinian monk and so, obviously, St Augustine's writings had a great influence on him. There is something about the idea of imitation that could lead to a sense of 'well, that's something we have to do, our effort, our intelligence will manage that'. The writings of Augustine would be concerned to remind us that without God we can do nothing, and our own efforts although they have their place, are as nothing compared to the love of God for us.

There comes a time in reading à Kempis when, of all Christian paradoxes, denial of self is the most difficult to understand. Surely God would not naturally will our pain and unpopularity. At the heart of the paradox lies the cross of Christ. That cross stands on Golgotha as a sign of the apparent failure of Jesus, where he was despised and rejected by the world. To imitate Christ is to be, at least, prepared for that cross, without at the same time losing a love for the world and for one's despisers. Thomas puts it like this: 'Grant that I may die to all things in this world, and for your sake love to be despised and unknown. Grant me, above all else to rest in you, that my heart may find its peace in you alone, *for you are the heart's true peace, its sole abiding place, and outside yourself all is hard and restless. In this true peace that is in you, the sole, supreme and eternal Good, I will dwell and take my rest.'*[11]

Perhaps we really only get to know another if we love them. Knowing can be a very clinical thing – knowing *about* someone – but the knowing we enter into through love is something much more profound, because we are changed by it and they are changed by it too. To pray through Christ to God, to ask Christ for his grace to dwell in us and to do only what is pleasing to him, is to forge a relationship of love. In love with Christ we begin to know his mind and he ours. We discover his mind is concerned about ours to the extent that he died for us. Knowing that about Christ is the first step to 'having the same mind' as his and so we too become those who are prepared to sacrifice ourselves for others in love. That doesn't sound quite like 'the rest' with which we left à Kempis, and yet to love another and give oneself for them is to find a peace within the struggle and the pain. For Christ, his death was the doing of the right thing, the loving thing, and as we enter into that death so we enter with him into the peace and rest of God.

***

St Francis of Assisi (1181/2–1226)

I dream of a mythic body,
Feathered and white, a landscape
                    horizoned and honed as an anchorite.
(Iacopo, hear me out, St Francis, have you a word for me?)
Umbrian lightfall, lambent and ichorous, mist through my days,
As though a wound, somewhere and luminous,
                              flickered and went out,
Flickered and went back out –
So weightless the light, so stretched and pained,
It seems to ooze, and then not to ooze, down from that one hurt.
You doubt it? Look. Put your finger there. No, there. You see?
                    from Charles Wright, 'Umbrian Dreams'.[12]

> Joy fall to thee, father Francis,
>   Drawn to the life that died;
> With the gnarls of the nails in thee, niche of the lance,
>   his
> Lovescape crucified.[13]
> from Gerard Manley Hopkins, 'The Wreck of the *Deutschland*'.

The friar who came to preach and whose friary was so much of a revelation to me all those years ago was a member of the Anglican Society of St Francis. This particular branch of the worldwide Franciscan family was founded between the two World Wars, partly as a response to the needs of the many 'wayfarers' who were seeking food, shelter and companionship, and partly as a result of a resurgence of interest in the example of St Francis himself. The many streams that flowed into the mighty river of Anglican Franciscan life are too numerous to mention here, but since the 1920s many personal lives, institutions and parishes have found their particular blend of evangelical Catholicism very attractive. It has served the Church at large extremely well. Behind it all lies the figure of the small man of Assisi. Francis Bernadone has been the guiding spirit, but that would be untrue to the real spirit of the movement. At the heart of Francis himself, and of Franciscans in general, is the person of Christ. Francis had a mind to imitate Christ. He took literally the evangelical counsels of his lord and master. The gospels were dynamite in his hands. Francis was concerned to live the life of Christ as closely as he could within the constraints of his times – twelfth-century Italy, not first century Judea. However, he did the best he possibly could to conform to his Master's commandments. There has not been anyone like Francis in the Western Church, and still the influence of Christ through his life attracts many followers. Some of these followers take vows and become Brothers or Sisters of the First Order of the Society of St Francis, some lead the contemplative life of the Poor Clares as part of the Second Order, and the Third Order or Tertiaries live their rule of life in the world. The Franciscan community stretches throughout the world as a part of both the Catholic and the Reformed traditions. It was in getting to know a little more about the contemporary life of the Franciscan tradition that I decided to visit Assisi in the holiday between finishing school and going to university. I set out on my own but met up with a friend in Genoa who was teaching English to the children of an Italian family. It was on this visit that we took the boat out to the island where St Francis spent the forty days of Lent and decided to spend the night in a deserted boathouse, rather than returning to the mainland. Every Lent I now recall that island and think of Francis thinking of Christ.

How do we write of the blessed Francis when he seemed to prefer not to write himself, except for a few prayers and ecstatic hymns. He preferred to write his own life on the wind, in the water and across the sky. He lived at a time when the idea of love was on everyone's lips, and wars were waged all around, and honour was upheld as a matter of course. It was in this context that he was moved to follow the call of Christ to rebuild the Church.

This he began literally with his own hands in a romantic gesture of love for the broken-down church of St Damian, just outside the walls of Assisi, stone upon stone. This literalism became Francis' way, his hallmark. He gave up everything, even at one point his clothes. He did this to follow Christ whose command was to sell all he had and give to the poor and follow him. So within the confines of the culture of thirteenth-century Italy, Francis entered on the Way at a very unsophisticated level; we would probably say, from the heart.

From the rebuilding of a broken-down church, he followed the Holy Spirit wherever it took him, as a soldier and troubadour for Christ. He took literally many of the commands in the gospels, even to the extent of being prepared to die in offering Christ to the Sultan of Babylon during the winter of 1219.

This story, and many others about St Francis, are to be found in *The Little Flowers of St Francis*. In some ways, the sentimental title in English is unfortunate. In Italian *Fioretti* can simply mean 'collection', and the stories although very readable and accessible, are not sentimental. The *Fioretti* draws on material from earlier sources, but has itself become one of the best-loved books of Christendom. The earliest manuscript of the *Fioretti* is dated 1396 and as usual with ancient books there is some dispute at to who compiled it. Fr Luke Wadding, the well-known Irish seventeenth-century author of *Annales Minorum* (1623), ascribed the whole work to Fra Ugolino da Santa Maria. Paul Sabatier on the other hand expresses the now general view that Fra Ugolino was not the author of all the chapters, but made careful selection and use of various earlier sources.

Keeping Christ's lenten fast

Just three events in Francis' amazing life (1181/2–1226) will have to suffice here as examples of the way in which he 'put on the mind of Christ'. When Jesus began his public ministry in Galilee, he went into a remote place for forty days and was tempted by Satan but, says the gospel, angels looked after him. Francis wished to follow his Master and imitate that forty-day fast.

> Since Saint Francis, the venerable servant of Christ, was in some ways almost like another Christ given to the world for the salvation of the people, God the Father willed that in many of his actions he should conform to and resemble His Son Jesus Christ. One Carnival Day (Shrove Tuesday) Saint Francis had gone to the Lake of Perugia (Lake Trasimeno) to visit the home of one of his disciples where he was to spend the night, and there he was inspired by God to observe Lent on an island in the lake. Finding no building where he could shelter, he went into a very dense thicket where thorns and other bushes formed a kind of arbour or grotto, and here he spent the time in prayer and contemplation of heavenly things. There he stayed throughout Lent eating and drinking nothing but half a small loaf. It is thought that Saint Francis consumed this out of reverence for the fast of Christ the Blessed, who fasted forty days and forty nights without taking any bodily sustenance. So by eating half of this loaf he avoided the venom of vainglory, and at the same time following the example of Christ.[14]

The gathering of brothers like the disciples

The next way in which Francis followed the example of Christ was in gathering together the venerable company of twelve companions. 'First let us consider how the glorious Saint Francis resembled Christ in every action of his life. For as at the beginning of his ministry Christ chose twelve apostles who were to renounce all worldly things and follow him in poverty and all virtues, so when Saint Francis founded his order, he chose twelve companions who took a vow of most noble poverty.'[15]

Like St Paul one of them was caught up into the third heaven – this was Br Giles. Another, Br Philip Lungo, was touched on the lips by an angel with burning coals. Br Sylvester spoke with God as friend to friend. Another, by the purity of his understanding, soared up into the light of divine wisdom like that eagle, John the evangelist: this was the very humble Br Bernard, who was a very profound exponent of holy scripture. Another was sanctified by God and canonized in heaven while still living in this world: this was Br Ruffino, a nobleman of Assisi.

We also read of Br Masseo, who was made by Francis to twirl round to see which way they should follow on the road. Br Simon was so holy he cast out the Devil by prayer. Br Conrad carried a leper fifteen miles between dawn and sunrise. Br John of La Verna received many graces from God, one of which was to enter into ecstasy when he contemplated the Body of Christ.

The stigmata, or sharing the wounds of Christ

The stigmata were the sacred wounds of Jesus Christ, which were miraculously imprinted on the body of St Francis in the year 1224 on the Feast of the Holy Cross (14 September) during his retreat on Mount La Verna. The description of the receiving of the wounds of Christ comes in the *Fioretti* under the title 'Five Considerations on the Holy Stigmata of Saint Francis: The Third Consideration: How the Stigmata were imprinted on Saint Francis.' We must assume that Francis had an intense and prolonged devotion to Christ in his passion on the cross. The suffering love of Christ and the compassion for the world that the crucifixion portrayed were both the visual images and the meditations that Francis would have been closest to. Francis is on the mountain of La Verna, and Br Leo is the reluctant witness.

Leo hears Francis repeating a prayer, 'Who art Thou, sweetest God? And what am I thy worthless servant?' This goes on through the night, and as the dawn rises on the Feast of the Holy Cross, another longer prayer is heard: 'My Lord Jesu Christ, I pray thee grant me two favours before I die: the first that during my lifetime I may feel in my own body, so far as is possible, the anguish which Thou, sweet Jesus, didst feel in the hour of thy most bitter Passion; the second that I may feel in my heart, so far as is possible the boundless love wherewith Thou, the Son of God wert moved, and willed to bear such agony for us sinners.'[16]

Then the seraph with six shining fiery wings descended from heaven which had the form of a man crucified and

> he felt great joy at the gracious face of Christ, who appeared to him so familiarly and looked on him so kindly; but seeing him nailed to the cross, he felt infinite sorrow and compassion. After a long period of secret converse this marvellous vision faded, leaving in the heart of Saint Francis a glowing flame of divine love, and in his body a wonderful image and imprint of the passion of Christ. For in the hands and feet of Saint Francis forthwith began to appear the marks of the nails in the same manner as he had seen them in the body of Jesus crucified. Similarly in his right side appeared an unhealed lance wound, red and bleeding, from which blood often flowed from the holy heart of Saint Francis, staining the habit and under-garment.[17]

Understanding this 'revelation' in purely scientific terms is doomed to failure. That it was real is more than likely. We perhaps can see it most helpfully as a sign of God's favour, as St Paul writes that he bears in his body the marks of Christ's suffering love. And again it is a case of being so at one with someone, in this case Christ, that we begin to resemble the one we love. The more we think on things, the more they become embedded in us, 'incarnate' we might say. We begin to share the attributes of what we consider. If we consider Christ in our thoughts and prayers, over the course of time, we shall in some way enter into the mystery of his being. Mystery is a good word for the relationship that was developing between Francis and Christ and can develop between Christ and us. Only certain sorts of language will have any hope of evoking the experience. Imagery helps us, because it links impossible things together. The seraphim have an imaginative reality; they are supernatural characters, each with six wings, which Isaiah saw standing above the throne of Yahweh (Isa. 6.2–7).

The seraphim were especially distinguished by the fervour of their love. Francis saw a vision in which a seraph and Christ were intertwined, indicating that Christ was all love and the great act of love on the cross transmitted itself from the spiritual realm into the bodily realm in the form of wounds, the wounds of love.

G. K. Chesterton put it like this in his biography of St Francis.

St Francis saw above him, filling the whole heavens, some vast immemorial unthinkable power, ancient like the Ancient of Days, whose calm men had conceived under the forms of winged bulls or monstrous cherubim, and all that winged wonder was in pain like a wounded bird. This seraphic suffering, it is said, pierced Francis' soul with a sword of grief and pity; it may be inferred that some sort of mounting agony accompanied the ecstasy. Finally after some fashion the apocalypse faded from the sky and the agony within subsided; and silence and the natural air filled the morning twilight and settled slowly in the purple chasms and cleft abysses of the Apennines.

The head of the solitary sank, amid all that relaxation and quiet in which time can drift by with a sense of something ended and complete; and as he stared downwards, he saw the marks of nails in his own hands.[18]

Francis had a particularly intimate relationship with the risen Christ, and received the graces that are the result of prayer, acts of love and obedience to the will of God. Francis entered into the mind and heart of Christ and perhaps most particularly in the bodiliness or incarnational aspect of Christ. So much so that Francis received the wounds of the passion in his own body. Francis must be one of the most Christ-like disciples of Christ since the apostolic age.

The particular aspect of joy that radiated from Francis, despite the physical hardships he endured as a result of his faith, can be seen as an aspect of love. Twelfth-century Italy was well known for its fierce internecine wars and its amorous passions. Francis channelled both aspects of these inherited traits into a sacrifice for Christ, putting himself at the disposal of Christ for the poor and the vulnerable. No task was done without joy, because in everything God was made manifest. Francis' songs and poems overflowed from a heart full of his love for all creatures and all manifestations of the creator, the greatest of whom was Jesus himself. Francis was a real troubadour for God.

Francis is thought by many to have been one of those whose mind, in Christian history, most closely reflected the mind of Christ. He didn't spend years at university reading the weighty tomes of the commentators. He turned his back on conventional Christianity and lived the demands of the gospel in a child-like way. He saw in Christ some basic principles of discipleship: love of the poor, a literal observance of the teachings of Jesus and the following of the way of the cross. The fruits of discipleship, what it meant to 'put on' the mind of Christ for St Francis, was a great sense of joy arising paradoxically out of giving up everything and depending on the providence of God to meet his daily needs. 'Give us this day our daily bread' really meant what it said and was prayed from the heart, and everything became gift.

We see in Francis that same wholehearted dependence on the Father that was Jesus' way, too. That intimate communication between God the creator and Francis mirrors Jesus' miraculous empathy with the natural world, which we call miracle. God provides food for the five thousand through the instigation of Jesus. 'The

Lord is my shepherd, I shall not want'. Francis and Jesus shared a mindset; it was faith in its absolute, uncompromising sense that links the two together. The bearing of the wounds of Christ on his body was a sign of the love that bonded the two. The marks of suffering love were a prize.

God gives us his saints to inspire us. He knows we are of limited imagination when it comes to following his Son. We thank him for providing such images of glory, hard won though they are. He knows we need friends on the journey who bear the likeness of Christ, who breathe out his joy and breathe in his love. In Francis we catch more than a glimpse of Christ.

Notes

1   Geoffrey Curtis C.R., *William of Glasshampton* (London: SPCK, 1947), p. 157.

2   R. George Thomas (ed), *The Collected Poems of Edward Thomas* (Oxford: Oxford University Press, 1978), p. 71.

3   Thomas à Kempis, *The Imitation of Christ* (Harmondsworth: Penguin Classics, 1952), p. 50.

4   Ibid., pp. 51–2.

5   Ibid., p. 52.

6   Ibid., p. 76.

7   Ibid., p. 91.

8   Ibid., p. 110.

9   Ibid., p. 83.

10 Rupert E. Davies, *Methodism* (Harmondsworth: Penguin Books, 1963), p. 90.

11 Thomas à Kempis, op. cit., p. 113.

12 Charles Wright, *Negative Blue* (Devon: Stride Publications, 2000), p. 102.

13 Gerard Manley Hopkins, *Poems and Prose* (Harmondsworth: Penguin Books, 1953), p. 20 (stanza 23 of 'The Wreck of the *Deutschland*').

14 *The Little Flowers of St Francis*, L. Sherley-Price (trans.) (Harmondsworth: Penguin Books, 1959), pp. 40–1.

15 Ibid., p. 25.

16 Ibid., p. 166.

17 Ibid., p. 166.

18 G.K. Chesterton, *St Francis of Assisi* (London: Hodder and Stoughton, 1923), pp. 151–2.

Chapter 3

The mind has mountains

Confronting the synoptic gospels

We have seen how the names of Jesus evoke worlds of meaning, and we have looked at two classic examples in Christian history of the way in which the life and example of Jesus has provided a basis for the spiritual lives of believers. Both were medieval examples. One was a book, *The Imitation of Christ*, and the other was a life gathered into a book, the *Fioretti*, although the relationship between book and life, as we shall see with Jesus, is always more complex than we think. As both *The Imitation* and the life of St Francis relate intimately to the life of Christ it is time to tread softly back into the core sources for that life, which are the gospels and the letters of Paul.

Home and school had brought me into contact with the name of Jesus. It began to be easier to say it to myself, but it was still difficult to share beyond that and to let out from its secret place. The time between school and university was spent in community service work in a school in Middlesex and an old people's home in Coventry. Being much more on my own and working out from my own resources, there was time and inclination for reflective prayer. The holy was slammed up against the extremely mundane and the physical. Stripping sodden beds, talking to the elderly, visiting the mentally ill with sixth-formers in a large Victorian-style asylum, and discovering the possibility of making deep friendships with some who had been in hospital most of their lives, was all part of life at that time. St Francis helped keep me close to Christ in all of this. He was the lens through which I glimpsed the Almighty in the ordinary and love was the name of Jesus at that time. It felt like some words that begin an eleventh-century hymn

'Jesu, dulcis memoria' ('Jesu, the very thought of thee'). St Bernard glosses them: 'You are good, O Lord to the soul who seeks you. If to the soul that seeks, how much more to the soul who finds? If the thought of you is sweet, how sweet must be your presence! If honey and milk is sweet beneath the tongue, what will it be *upon* the tongue?'[1]

Along with a growing confidence in owning the name of Jesus came something altogether more complex. It was called 'theology' and I could not say it turned me upside down but nothing on the intellectual level could be simple any more and it seemed there would never be an end to the process of discovery. In the 1960s it seemed that nothing could be said for certain about Jesus. All we could say was 'that's what it says in Matthew, but it doesn't say it in Mark'. In each case truth needed to survive on its own integrity. If it seemed to be true, if it was authentic, if it didn't have too much suspicion of it being made up for a purpose, then it could hold, but we certainly could not believe anything lightly. We had to keep checking the small print and doing that was fascinating but it did not make for simple Christianity and it didn't make for easy 'imitation'. For if we were to copy Christ, which Christ should we copy: Mark's, Matthew's, Luke's, John's, or Paul's?

It wasn't the role of the university theology department to choose for us. The academic task was to show us bits of the engine, name them, usually in German, give the ability to take the engine apart, put it back together again, and leave it at that. Faith would be dissected but it often seemed to be dead on the slab before we could make the first incision. Surprisingly, I am now very glad about that. I found it frustrating at the time but over the years I have been able to use those critical tools to fashion a stronger faith, or at least to fashion a relationship with Christ which is not blind to the enigmatic nature of the sources. It was also possible for the myriad of clues that then seemed so jumbled to settle into a meaning interesting enough, beautiful enough, tough enough, for me to feel committed to the Christ who lies enigmatically behind them all.

We begin to love the name that others scorn or disregard. It is sweet upon our lips and in our hearts. The name matters and can no longer be sworn without a second thought, without knowing all that it means in terms of sacrifice, love, forgiveness, tenderness and healing. We become marked by the name. It grows within us. We take on the name, not easily said, as some might suppose, because with the love comes the demand. At times it seems so easy and at others seems so hard. The name of Jesus Christ both comforts and challenges us.

Knowing that the gospels are a complex mixture of materials, which start at different distances from the situations they describe, makes the task of assessing the mind of Christ not less but more interesting. Seeing Christ through a particular lens, say the lens of Luke, gives us the task of assessing what purpose lay behind his choice of story, of words, and in the placing of material. That doesn't make it any the less true. Each section has to be seen on its own merits and with its own literary as well as its own 'real' history.

But first I had to learn that the gospels of Matthew, Mark and Luke are called the synoptic gospels because they share a similar pattern or synopsis of the life of Jesus. John's gospel is meditative and idiosyncratic, at times intensely detailed and at others it contemplates the nature of God in Jesus Christ from the mystic's perspective. Consequently the 'synoptics' are dealt with separately, acknowledging too that John is in many cases dependent on the others. Each of the four gospels has its own particular style. There are differences in the content, depending on the information that was available to the evangelist, but there are also differences in the way they present that information. As a result, the picture we get of Jesus is broadly the same across the four gospels, but the subtle emphases are highly illuminating.

The question remains, if we are to put on the mind of Christ, whose interpretation of that mind do we follow, if all the gospels have different emphases? Do we put on the Christ of the Markan enigma, the teacher of Matthew's gospel, the good and holy man of Luke, or the otherworldly figure of John's gospel? As we enter into each gospel and in each weigh all the evidence that they give us, what is the process we use for assessing what we might call 'the real Christ', with the greatest attention to the truth that the gospel records can give us?

That process must begin by entering imaginatively into the world of each of the gospels separately, questioning all the time why it was written like it was. This can be a painful stage because it can seem rather detached from faith, but eventually the cultural and religious setting of each gospel becomes clearer. Then we can begin to see the patterns and central features emerging, such as the teaching, the crucifixion, the place of the disciples, the resurrection, and perhaps most important of all the relationship of Christ to his Father. Then, when we have seen what is fundamental to them all, we can begin to enter into these matters that were closest to Christ's purpose and see them more from the inside than as on-lookers. We identify with Christ at the points which were for him the most crucial, and by doing so put on his way of being, his mind.

Through the spiritual pain barrier of absorbing these texts, and indeed coming to find them luminous in the search for the mind of Christ, we can then begin to understand that putting on the mind of Christ is not like putting on a mask or a costume, something external or superimposed on our inner selves; putting on the mind of Christ transforms us from the very centre of our being, from the point where the very springs of hope and love and faith are born. It is from this point, difficult to place biologically, that we are transformed. I suspect it is the place we have come to call the 'soul', drawing on all that the heart can give and all that the mind can do; we become transformed into the likeness of Christ.

The gospels help us on our way with this. They help hugely. They have a converting power, because they describe the one who had in his lifetime and now eternally the power to transform lives. Sitting in a Crusaders' class hearing the leader explain the text 'whatever you do for the least of these my brethren you do for me' (Mt. 25.40), and then going up and asking him for his autograph was all part of this. To which he said, 'can you lend me your book for the week and I'll do a special entry for you', which he did, most spectacularly. He brought it back with the text beautifully written, and the heraldic Crusaders' badge above it. And the 'brethren' he had been talking about were the poor, the hungry, and the lonely. I didn't then know the differences between the gospels, so the words had the power to affect me on a level far distant from 'the close reading of the text'. That was life changing then, but there were more changes to come, and there were riches to discover in attending closely to the gospels.

The aim of these following investigations into the gospels is, with a broad brushstroke, to trace the way in which the presentation of Jesus by the evangelists has led to the formation of certain spiritual traditions. It may be complicating matters hugely to insist on a shift in thought that prises Jesus away from the text and allows us to see a fault line between the 'authentic' Jesus as he would have been if we had met him in 30 AD and the Jesus of the gospels. Between the life and the gospels there was a process of interpretation orchestrated by the evangelists as they handled sources which they drew on to flesh out their gospels and create the good news for the communities they were writing for.

The interpretations make it more not less exciting, because we get the story of the impression Jesus made upon his earliest followers and learn what they found important, helpful, intriguing, life changing and frustrating about him. No history is free of interpretation. The way we engage with those who in turn engaged with Jesus sets up all sorts of mental and spiritual vibrations. If we can cope with those vibrations and enjoy them, then theology comes alive and we cease to be frustrated by imagining there is a final answer other than that which sets up a creative relationship between ourselves and the Jesus of history.

Mark and the centrality of faith
(Biblical references will refer to Mark's gospel unless otherwise stated.)

In Mark, Jesus requests that the people hear the gospel of God: 'The time is fulfilled and the Kingdom of God has come near; repent, and believe the good news' (1.15). Jesus is asking people to look away from himself and listen to the proclamation that will save them from an approaching disaster. He is like the captain of a sinking ship who is ordering his crew (the disciples) and the people (the crowds) onto the lifeboats and this captain is showing people how best to save themselves.

'He appointed twelve...to be with him and to be sent out to proclaim the message, and to have authority to cast out demons (3.14). Twelve men are appointed. They are like Jesus, in that they carry the same message and are given the power to heal and there is a third thing they share with Jesus, which is knowledge of the secret of the kingdom of God. Having the secret, being in on the mystery of what the kingdom is and how it is accessed, is to be as intimately connected with the way God works as it is possible to be. Privately to his disciples 'he explained everything' (4.34).

So the teacher chooses twelve disciples who could be like him and teach God's commands, proclaim the good news and suffer with him. But no sooner does he attempt to initiate the disciples into the mystery of his way than the disciples demonstrate a complete lack of faith. It is faith they lack rather than knowledge. Faith is the essential element of being 'like Christ'. If the disciples are to put on Christ's mind they have to begin with faith. They have to 'believe the gospel', but the disciples fall short in both faith and trust in Jesus. They panic in the storm on the lake (4.35–40). Jesus said, 'have you still no faith?' Jesus returns to his home in Nazareth and 'was unable to perform any miracle there', because of the people's lack of faith. They admired his wisdom to begin with, but with lack of faith they turned against Jesus. The disciples did not understand the incident of the loaves, for their minds were closed (6.51–2). They were as dull as the rest about what was clean and unclean (7.18). Peter set his mind on human things and not on the things of God (8.33). Peter, James and John seem bemused by the transfiguration of Jesus (9, passim).

The disciples left at the foot of the mountain are unable to cure the boy possessed by demons and Jesus implies that they didn't have the necessary capacity of prayer to make the miracle possible. James and John ask if they can sit beside Jesus in the kingdom (10.36f.) not realizing that this was impossible. The disciples are unable to stay awake in Gethsemane. Judas betrays Jesus. Peter denies Jesus and in the end all the disciples slip away into the night, never again to appear in the gospel. If it is correct that the boy who fled naked from the garden was Mark himself, then he was in a very good position to know the fickle nature of the disciples' commitment, for he himself must have felt it. Even the witness of the women at the resurrection is in doubt, because they ran away from the tomb 'afraid' and fear in the gospel is the opposite of faith and so is tantamount to unbelief.

It is abundantly clear from this most original and formative of gospel records that Jesus would have wanted his disciples to be like him, to share the strength of faith that allowed healing to take place, and cold and stony hearts to be turned. The disciples' response was far from adequate. However, we do get a very strong sense that Jesus had the power and authority to be able to proclaim God's kingdom through word and deed. On the cross there was a titanic struggle going on between faith and doubt. Yet the resurrection and Jesus' appearance to the women vindicate what was clear throughout the gospel, that Jesus was the only one through whom this faith was to be handed on, first to his followers and then, by implication, to us.

The supreme agent of communication in the gospels is generally the Holy Spirit. After the death of Jesus, faith was inspired by the Holy Spirit and this is described at length in the gospel of Luke and the Acts of the Apostles. For Mark the Holy Spirit is present at two key points in the gospel. First the Holy Spirit is at work in the baptism of Jesus. Before the baptism, John the Baptist proclaims to the people 'I have baptized you with water: but he (the one who is more powerful than I) will baptize you with the Holy Spirit' (1.10). Then, at the moment of baptism Jesus saw 'the heavens torn apart and the Spirit descending like a dove on him'. After the baptism 'the Spirit immediately drove him out into the wilderness' (1.12).

Just before the passion, Jesus speaks privately to Peter, James, John and Andrew, and forewarns them, 'When they bring you to trial and hand you over, do not worry beforehand about what you are to say; but say whatever is given you at the time, for it is not you who speak, but the Holy Spirit' (13.11). These are modest glimpses of the work and influence of the Spirit. However, for Luke interpreting the primitive gospel of Mark in slightly more leisured times the Holy Spirit is the means of awakening and strengthening the key personal gift of Jesus to his disciples, and that gift was faith.

This remarkable gospel is cut short. The most ancient text concludes at 16.8 with the words 'they (the women) said nothing to anyone for they were afraid . . .' One authority concludes the book with an additional shorter ending; others include the additional shorter ending and then continue with verses 9–20, which are printed in most translations but are later additions. Mark's gospel begins with Christ's adult ministry and ends with an empty tomb and some traumatized women. The abbreviated end could be the result of the Roman soldiers coming to arrest Mark and Mark quickly hiding his manuscript; or it could be a lost page or two; or it could be that Mark wanted to invite people to find the conclusion in a re-reading of the text and to find the answers there. The answers to the question 'Do you believe that this apparent failure is the Son of God, the risen Christ?', is a matter for faith. This is Mark's great subject, which each of us has to accept for ourselves; no amount of physical evidence will encourage us to make the blind leap of faith into accepting 'Jesus as Lord'. The disciples fell short. They abandoned Jesus on the cross. Will we? Do we? Or will we believe and find in Christ the secret to the kingdom of God?

Is not the end of Mark's gospel to be found in the passionate concern for 'faith' in the gospel of John, and also in the pastoral theology of Paul? Both writers go some way to explaining the mechanism of faith, what it is, what it does, where it comes from. Paul uses the noun 'faith' 123 times in his extant letters, and that does not include Hebrews, Ephesians, or Colossians. John prefers the verb 'believing' and uses it 100 times in his gospel. If we are to look for who picked up the torch from Mark on the issue of faith as the key factor in Jesus' teaching, we must look to Paul and John. If 'faith' is the key factor in Jesus' teaching, then to be like him and to frame our lives, heart, mind and soul on his example, 'faith' is the place to discover the secret. This was the secret that the disciples in Mark's gospel found it too hard to fathom. It is as though the last page of the gospel is torn off and we have to write it ourselves, in the shape our lives take in response to Jesus' call for faith. The gospel ends, 'for they were afraid', but we who know the whole story, we must carry the torch, and persist in faith.

Matthew and the sermon on the mount
(Biblical references will be to Matthew's gospel unless otherwise stated.)

All the gospel writers are editors. Matthew is more of an editor than most. He gathers a whole variety of material together. He has on the desk in front of him material already used by Mark and a document known to both Matthew and Luke, which both make use of in subtly different ways. In addition, Matthew has had access to material which only he saw fit to use, in the description, for example, of the circumstances surrounding Jesus' birth (the astrologers) and in places he reworked the basic narratives of the crucifixion and the resurrection appearances.

We are dealing in Matthew with a patchwork, not a garment woven throughout, and so to find a simple thread of tradition from which has come one single formative spiritual tradition is difficult. However, distinct parts of Matthew do help us locate a significant and unique view of Jesus. If we plunge into the gospel of Matthew at chapter five we shall find a uniquely influential piece of teaching, shaped into eight affirmations of the blessed nature of certain categories of people. These affirmations are part of a larger section in Matthew's gospel known as 'The Sermon on the Mount'.

A short section of that (5.1–10) begins the Sermon and repeats the word 'blessed' at the beginning of each line. This would suggest that these 'beatitudes' (Latin: beatus) written in an incantatory mode, were perhaps used as part of the worship of the Church. The genius, the Christ-like nature of them, emerges in their radical overturning of the traditional understanding of 'happiness', which would have included wealth, success, a luxurious life, worldly glory and military honour. To follow the inspiration of the beatitudes is to follow Christ's radical alternative to that understanding of happiness.

The specific moral thrust of the beatitudes gives them a universal quality, which does not depend initially on a knowledge of Jesus to make sense of them. These precepts stand on their own. Mahatma Gandhi was influenced by them. After an initial dislike of Christianity because of the experience he had of missionaries heaping abuse on Hindus and their gods, one thing took root in him. That was the conviction that morality was the basis of things and that truth was the substance of all morality.

Blessed are the poor in spirit ...
The poor (the Hebrew 'avi') described the literally poor whom the worldly rich despised and persecuted. The poor are frequently mentioned in the Psalter as those whom the Lord addressed and who were despised by the recognized pious of the day. Such were the truly pious ones, not outwardly and conventionally, but 'in their spirit'. So these 'poor' were destitute of the wealth of learning and intellectual culture that the rabbinic schools were proud of. It was from the poor that Jesus gained his following. His teaching and his way of preaching attracted them. Jesus said 'thank you Lord of heaven and earth, for hiding these things from the learned and wise and revealing them to the simple'. Paul wrote in 1 Cor. 1.26, 'Not many of you were wise by any human standards ... but God chose what is foolish in the world to shame the wise; God chose what is weak in the world to shame the strong'.
      ... and theirs is the kingdom of heaven.

Blessed are those who mourn ...
The word 'sorrowful' was most frequently used for mourning the dead, and for the sorrows and sins of others. The letter of James picks this up, 'Be sorrowful, mourn and weep. Turn your laughter into mourning and your gaiety into gloom. Humble yourselves before God and he will lift you high.'

Is the state of sorrow blessed in itself, or is it just that if we are sorrowful then that makes us open to receive the comfort of Christ? It is too easy to imagine that all the great Christians down the centuries have been constantly 'happy'. That is too simple. At the heart of this sorrow is an openness to the pain of the world and to God's remedy for pain, to mourning over the power of evil in the world, and to claiming God's victory over it.

> Those who sow in tears
> will reap in joy.
> He who goes out weeping
> carrying his bags of seed
> will come back with shouts of joy
> bearing their sheaves with them.
> (Ps. 126.6–7)

Christianity is not a system into which we have to fit the awkward fact of pain: it is itself one of the awkward facts which have to be fitted into any system we make . . . If any message from the core of reality ever were to reach us, we should expect to find it in just that unexpectedness, that wilful, dramatic anfractuosity (awkwardness) which we find in the Christian faith. It has the master touch, the rough taste of reality, not made by us, or, indeed, for us, but hitting us in the face.[2]

. . . and they will be comforted.

Blessed are the meek . . .
'The humble shall inherit the land' (Ps. 37.11). Jesus came among the people as 'gentle and humble hearted' (11.29), 'gentle and riding on an ass' (21.5). Peter's letter says 'your beauty should reside in the inmost centre of your being . . . a gentle spirit.' The image of 'gentle Jesus, meek and mild' is not an attractive one. It lacks a sense of determination and toughness in faith that Jesus showed and lavishing virtue after virtue on Jesus, as if he had to possess every conceivable quality of goodness recommended in the New

Testament, drains the humanity out of him. To be gentle, paradoxically, takes toughness. A lot of restraint has to be exercised to achieve a measure of gentleness.

Sensitivity is a stronger contemporary word to describe Jesus' ability to feel for the particular needs of a person in the crowd. We think of the woman who touched the hem of his garment. We think of Jesus' approach to Jairus' daughter and the way he dealt with the woman caught in adultery. In addition we remember his non-retaliation at his arrest, trial and crucifixion.

... and they will inherit the earth.

Blessed are those who hunger and thirst to see right prevail ...
We are never far in the beatitudes from the practical outworking of a deep spirituality. There is no hiding in a cocoon of holiness. Engaged with the painful and complex issues of human decision-making, behaviour, community action, and all the frustrations that go with having to put into practice a spiritual agenda, what is right? What was right in the mind of Christ?

The long tradition of 'righteousness' is probably our best clue here. The righteous person was the one who observed the laws, both divine and human, someone who was upright, virtuous and kept the commands of God. Paul was just such a man and his example is formative. He was a good man and a just man within the understanding of the Hebrew law, but more was expected of him following the call from Christ. Righteousness needs to go beyond the keeping of the law. It had to go the extra mile and involved sacrifice, hunger and thirst. It was in fact impossible to be perfectly righteous and so the love and mercy of God had to come and rescue us, complete what we could not manage, and the one to do that was Christ.

At the baptism, when John would have prevented Jesus from being baptized, Jesus said to John: 'It is proper for us in this way to fulfil all righteousness'. So John consented to perform a baptism for Jesus for the washing away of sins. Righteousness, doing the right thing, was a priority for Jesus and he would have had that very much in mind when he said: 'Unless your righteousness exceeds that of the scribes and Pharisees, you will never enter the Kingdom of heaven' (5.20). Jesus was dedicated in his commitment to righteousness and understood that living righteously meant more than just words. It meant deeds. His most righteous act was an offering of sacrifice for the failure of righteousness and 'there was no other good enough to do it'.

... and they will be filled.

Blessed are the merciful ...

In one of the parables of Matthew's gospel a master releases a servant from a huge debt. That servant, having been shown mercy by his master, then demands a huge repayment from a fellow servant who is unable to pay. The master hears of this and punishes the original servant for his failure to show mercy, in the way he himself had been shown mercy (18.23–35).

The merciful are those who do not, for the sake of a greater virtue, and in certain circumstances, demand their full rights. Mercy is on a different plane from the law. It demands from us different priorities. It is a blessing and an unexpected act of loving-kindness. It is out of the ordinary and cannot be automatically expected. As Portia says in the *Merchant of Venice* it is like the rain, it comes when it comes and we give thanks for it. Mercy does not work to fixed laws, other than the law of God's love. So we cry '*Kyrie eleison*, Lord, have mercy!' as the blind man did who followed Jesus and sought to have his sight back (9.27) and the Canaanite woman whose daughter was tormented by a demon (15.22), and the man with the epileptic son (17.17). Mercy is God's healing power of love, which works through his Son, and we are given a share of that mercy partly to give us health and wholeness, and partly to offer the same back, in whatever way we can, to those in need. Who cries 'mercy!' to us, and do we hear and respond?

... and they will receive mercy.

Blessed are the pure in heart ...

We often think of purity in the outward acts and substances of life, especially water, for washing, keeping clean and free from disease. Yet the purity of the beatitudes is the purity and cleanliness within the heart and mind. It lies at the source and spring of our being, within our hearts and minds, and if the source is pure then the stream has a chance of being pure too. 'Those who have clean hands and a pure heart...shall receive a blessing from the Lord' (Ps. 24.4). 'Make me a clean heart, O God, and renew a right spirit within me.' (Ps. 51.10).

There was in Christ nothing impure or unclean, yet that was not because he had no contact with impurity, as it was understood in those days. Illness and disease had the stigma of uncleanness then, and Jesus moved among the sick, touching them and being touched by them. Every rule of purity must have been breached by the events surrounding the crucifixion and yet the essential purity of intention remained intact. Purity of heart is to will one thing and Christ's one thing was to will the will of God.

...and they shall see God.

Blessed are the peacemakers...
These are banner headlines for the peace movement, but what sort of peace is being thought about here? Are we to understand this as peace between the nations, brokering peace deals, painstakingly assisting the process towards peaceful coalition for warring factions throughout the world? That would be a good thing and the spectre of Mahatma Gandhi rises into the mind again. We can spend so much time on existential realities, peace in the heart, that we can forget how much the wars of the world disrupt and destroy the possibility of all the benefits that come from peace. The peacemakers, those who dedicate their lives to drawing the best out of people and bringing them together to experience peace, and so to long for it and work for it, are a great gift to the world.

However, this word 'peacemakers' is a unique word in the gospels. The phrase 'to make peace' is also very rare. Its one use is when the writer of the Letter to the Colossians wants to describe what Christ did on the cross in obedience to God. In Christ 'God was pleased to reconcile to himself all things, whether on earth or in heaven, by making peace through the blood of his cross' (Col. 1.20). This peacemaking is concerned with the bringing together into unity of all things. It is a vision of perfection, completeness, unity, which is hard to imagine as a reality in this world. Yet what the writer holds out is the reality of an example of unity which exists in Christ and waits patiently through the ages for its completion in this world.

> *...and they will be called children of God.*

Blessed are those who are persecuted for righteousness' sake ...
Working to bring in the Kingdom of God inevitably meant persecution and hardship. The disciples were sent out as sheep in the midst of wolves, and had to expect to be 'dragged before governors and kings' because of their allegiance to Jesus, 'and as a testimony to the Gentiles'. 'Do not fear those who kill the body but cannot kill the soul; rather fear him who can destroy both body and soul in hell' (10.24f.).

Dietrich Bonhoeffer sent a brief meditation on 'The Suffering of the Righteous' from Tegel Prison on 8 June 1944 to Eberhard and Renate Bethge. He headed it with two quotations: Psalm 34.19 'The righteous person must suffer many things, but the Lord delivers him out of them all' and 1 Peter 3.9 'Repay not evil with evil or railing with railing, but rather bless, and know that you are called to this, so that you should inherit the blessing.'

Bonhoeffer continued, 'The answer of the righteous person to the sufferings which the world cause her is to bless. That was the answer of God to the world, which nails Christ to the cross: blessing. God does not repay like with like, and neither should the righteous person. No condemning, no railing, but blessing.'[3]

> *...and theirs is the Kingdom of Heaven.*

Many other matters, of course, are related in Matthew's gospel – remarkable parables of judgement and mercy – but it is in this core section of the Sermon on the Mount that we find the unique teaching charisma of the Matthean Christ. The Sermon on the Mount reflects the great gift of the commandments to Moses on Mount Sinai. Matthew's sermon in chapter five begins with these beatitudes and they provide the most radical manifesto of all time, set against the massively overbearing dictates of the Jewish law at the time of Christ. The beatitudes look a little like poetry in the way they are set out, and there is the constant refrain 'blessed are . . .', but the demands are revolutionary. They turn the normal expectation of the law on its head. They come from the underside up, and not top down. It is the poor who are blessed, the least likely and therefore the most likely to win the praise of God. This is the new radical law that put Moses on the mountain in a completely new light. This is the *new* Decalogue, and the *new* covenant.

The categories of the blessed are so powerfully resonant of the mind of Christ. Who else would elevate the poor and the weak but the one who saw in children the face of God and heard the cries of beggars and noticed the widow's penny. If we want to know what and who Christ had on his heart we need to go again to this most famous list: the poor in spirit, those who mourn, the meek, those who hunger and thirst for righteousness, the merciful, the peacemakers, those who are persecuted for righteousness, and the reviled.

Luke: chapter ten
(References are to Luke 10 unless otherwise stated)

With a more analytical approach to the gospels, rather than a devotional one, we can begin to see patterns of thought and interpretation. We look first at the shape of the passage and recognize that there are blocks of material that have a common theme. For example, the gospel of Luke, like Matthew, soon takes us into the story of the birth of Jesus. You might think that would be obvious, but neither Mark nor John begin that way. Luke's narrative is a unique construction giving us information that is nowhere else to be found.

These days, the story of the birth of our children is highly significant. Character is formed even before birth. The environment into which a child is born, the nature of the early bonding and so on, all go to make up the picture of a distinctive human being. In a fascinating way Luke's gospel gives us a similar emphasis, but

with quite a different atmosphere. The place of miracle and wonder is all important: a virgin birth, the appearance of the angels,
'glory shines all about' and at the still centre a virgin betrothed to
a man named Joseph. We should be in no doubt that God is doing
something very special indeed in giving the world a Saviour, but
one who is born into a humble environment, devout, and open to
the influences of the long history of Jewish faith.

The mind of Christ is formed, in Luke's gospel, by the traditions
of his parents. The family go to and from Jerusalem for religious
ceremonies, purification, circumcision, and the annual visit for the
Passover festival. Chapters one and two of Luke's gospel prepare
the way for Jesus to lead a life that is devoted to the ways of God
and to teaching the ways of God to an emerging community of
believers.

Chapter three takes up the story, as all four gospels do, with the
entrance into a ministry, a calling that has begun at the door of
baptism. However, rather than taking a broad look over the whole
gospel, what if we were to take a sample from one area of the
gospel, one chapter, to see how the gospel works in depth, much
as a soil scientist might probe deep into the earth to check what is
happening at different levels.

Chapter ten is something of a half-way point in the gospel and
gives us an opportunity to see what variety of material Luke is
dealing with and how that material relates to the way Christ is
thinking and through that insight to shape our own discipleship
in his Spirit, to put on his mind about things. We should expect
some difference in cultural attitudes from our own, but again we
shall be able to see where those differences find some resolution
in Christ.

The Lord has appointed 70 others to go ahead in pairs to every place that he was hoping to go to proclaim the coming of the
kingdom of God, and this they do. The going out and the coming
back are documented, but we hear little of the details of where
they went, who they stayed with, and exactly what they did. One
detail only is reported, 'Lord, in your name even the demons submit to us'. Jesus' attitude to the mission is couched in the language

of quite severe condemnation. The 70 go out with this ringing in their ears: 'Woe to you, Chorazin! Woe to you, Bethsaida! [villages on the edge of the Sea of Galilee]. For if the deeds of power done in you had been done in Tyre and Sidon, they would have repented long ago, sitting in sackcloth and ashes. But at the judgement it will be more tolerable for Tyre and Sidon than for you. And you, Capernaum,

will you be exalted to heaven?
No, you will be brought down to Hades.' (vv. 13–15)

This material is full of judgement and strange to ears formed by an understanding of a gentle Jesus. It is hard material to hear, hard-edged, and the very opposite of sentimental. When the 70 return, it is as though Jesus knew exactly all that had happened. 'I watched Satan fall from heaven like a flash of lightning' (v. 17). This again, though exhilarating, is strange material. It makes us conscious of a wide cultural gap between ways of thinking in our own sophisticated Western society and the mental world in which demons are a metaphor for evil. We do indeed feel this powerful influence in the world today, but prefer to describe it in the language of psychology. We get a glimpse here of the important apocalyptic traditions within the Judaism of the day, with which Jesus was obviously familiar.

'Devil' and 'demon' language was commonplace in Jesus' day and we may feel uncomfortable with it. Our equivalent might be to speak of 'evil'. Both types of language conjure up fear and grief; we may well be seeing things in a rather similar way. Against this culture of demons, Jesus sets the kingdom of God. For Jesus the concept of the kingdom seems to have been as real as things can get. The language he used is of inhabiting that kingdom, going to it and it coming nearer and being able to share space with God and others in it. This kingdom is coming near and it will come on a day soon.

Managing the language of what we might conceive of as abstract or metaphorical, but which Jesus understood as real, spatially

and in time, is one of the major challenges in reading the New
Testament. It reaches into the very heart of the resurrection itself. It leaves many struggling with a bi-focal vision in which we
continually have to do mental gymnastics to say what something
is, in another's currency and thought world. We want to feel what
things were like in another's head, how they judged reality and
empathize with that, and yet we also have to make decisions about
language on the basis of what might be accessible to others. Are we
literally out to discover the demons and get them to submit to us?
Or are we in situations of mission and outreach trying to discern
the equivalent 'demons' in terms we may feel more comfortable
with, e.g. the demon of greed, the demon of cruelty and violence,
and the demon of despair?

'I have given you authority to tread on snakes and scorpions, and
over all the power of the enemy, and nothing will hurt you.' (v. 19).
This sounds very literal and out of it has come a long tradition,
including that of St Francis of Assisi, which sees creation as part of
God's very being, and therefore God has the power to pacify and
mollify what some consider harmful aspects of creation like snakes
and scorpions. There is a truth in that. Some people are given the
gift to live as if Eden was restored in a practical way today. Yet,
again, there is a good reason why we should feel free to translate
snakes and scorpions as metaphors of all that tempts us into evil.

***

The chapter continues (vv. 20–23) with a collage of material that is
highly reminiscent of the language of John (vv. 21–22) and then of
Mark (v. 23). Luke was a great gatherer of material and so perhaps
it is not surprising that we have these influences coming in. It is a
glorious accolade of praise that incorporates both the Holy Spirit
and the Father and was therefore an ideal text for understanding
the nature of Jesus as one of a family of three: Father, Son and
Holy Spirit. It is quite strange that what is so difficult to translate
into contemporary terms when it is part of Jesus' experience of the
demonic, becomes much easier to accept when it refers to the Holy

Spirit. Although, looking at it objectively, both areas are couched in metaphorical terms. Perhaps it is because, speaking personally, one feels on safer ground with God than with demons. Get the demons wrong and they will come back to bite. Get God wrong and by his nature revealed in Christ he would be forbearing enough to give us another chance.

In this one short chapter ten, so far, we have seen Christ as exorcist, mission leader, and prophet. Now the gospel shifts its tone and Luke is about to link the mission of the 70, the victory over the demons, and Jesus' prayer to the Father (concerning the hiding of mysteries from the wise and the revealing of them to children) with a parable that sums up everything that is Christ-like.

It is Luke's editorial creativity that sets the bell tolling about the concern of the Father to teach the children, when he says in his prayer to the Father 'I thank you because you have hidden these things from the wise and intelligent and have revealed them to infants' (v. 21). What better way of showing that than by a story and not just any story but one which has entered the hearts and minds of generations, the Parable of the Good Samaritan (vv. 25–37).

So Luke recounts the parable of Jesus in the context of a question to Jesus from a lawyer. The lawyer asks, 'Who is my neighbour?' A story speaks to the childlike quality in all of us. We can all understand and feel for a man who is robbed and left for dead at the side of a road and can all be surprised that the one who comes to help is the one who we least expected to do so. No one tells the story better than the story tells itself. On the level of telling it is self-explanatory, but bears all the hallmarks of Christ's mind.

The lead-in to the story was a discussion between prophet and lawyer, between a teacher and the one who had all the answers. Jesus overturns expectations. All we need to know about a Samaritan is that it was out of character for him to help an injured man. The one who was himself considered by society as the outcast was the one to help the wounded outcast on that busy thoroughfare between Jerusalem and Jericho. This was a road that Jesus knew well.

Then there was the super abundance of charity by the Samaritan, taking the man to the inn, promising to pay more if needed when he returned, echoing the extra mile that Jesus had asked his disciples to go. If nothing else of the gospel survives that would be enough. It is a perfect example of sacrificial love and it is totally unexpected. The listeners are left thinking, which one of the three that were walking along the road is me and which one would I like to be? But Christ is not just a storyteller. He moves from story to the moment of truth. He comes out of the world of fiction and into the world of reality. The lawyer knows the right answers, he is the educated person and he is also sympathetic to the spirit of the story, but the ring of the final words must have haunted him, as they haunt us, 'Go and do likewise'.

There are moments like this in the gospels when we sense a palpable silence. The rich young ruler ponders Jesus' words, 'Go, sell all you have and give to the poor.' The woman caught in adultery cannot believe her luck and is stunned by being given a second chance, 'Go away and sin no more.' This is the voice more than any other that leads us to the mind of Christ: definite, compassionate, transforming and 'full of grace and truth'.

Joachim Jeremias in his book on The Parables of Jesus says, 'In attempting to recover the original significance of the parables, one thing above all becomes evident: it is that all the parables of Jesus compel his hearers to come to a decision about Jesus' purpose and mission. For the parables are full of 'the secret of the Kingdom of God'.[4] Those whom Jesus confronted with the parables experienced the kingdom in their midst. Jesus' parables allowed the kingdom of God to break into this world and still do so in our present circumstances.

One more section remains of this chapter of Luke's gospel (vv. 38–42), and it is a vignette of the domestic life of Martha and Mary. It is a theme that runs through the gospels and it is about attentive listening. It will lead on in chapter eleven to Jesus' teaching of the Lord's prayer to the disciples and so is well placed. Martha is distracted by her many tasks. Mary sits at the feet of Jesus and listens to him (v. 39). Jesus is the teacher and Mary the listener. The final words of the Parable of the Good Samaritan which precede the Mary and Martha incident are 'Go and do likewise.' They provide the silent refrain for this passage too. Luke the teacher, always keen to press his point, offers his readers 'the one thing needful', which is listening to the Lord and going and doing 'likewise'.

Mission, the encouragement of the Holy Spirit, the secret of sacrificial love and listening to the Lord, is the rich fare of one chapter of Luke's gospel. Luke shares with Matthew a teaching brief, writing for the emerging Church which is eager to know about the life of Christ. Luke's companion Paul was formulating his ideas about the significance of Christ. Luke himself was dealing with the narrative, the story, and the memories of the Galilean disciples. Some are theologians, some are artists, and some agonize over the secret of the kingdom of God. Such are the 'synoptic gospels' as they reflect the moral, apocalyptic and pastoral influences of Christ on the emerging Christian Church. We wait on John to provide the final imaginative meditations on the details, which perhaps he knew first hand, and perhaps he did not. Whichever, John will be the subject of the final chapter of this book.

Notes

1   F.J.E. Raby, *A History of Christian-Latin Poetry* (Oxford: Clarendon Press, 1927), p. 330.
2   C.S. Lewis, *The Problem of Pain*, (London: The Centenary Press, 1940), p. 12.
3   Dietrich Bonhoeffer, *Meditating on the Word* (Cambridge, MA: Cowley Publications, 1986), pp. 98–9.
4   Joachim Jeremias, *The Parables of Jesus* (London: SCM Press Ltd, 1954), p. 159.

Chapter 4

But we have the mind of Christ

Faith

We have spent time looking at the synoptic gospels and later in this chapter we turn to Paul, but not without first discovering a bridge between the gospels and the letters of Paul. They are often separated. Some tend to love the particularity of the gospels and fear the abstractions of the letters, while others know Paul's letters as the source of the awakening of their faith and feed on his theology. That seems an unfortunate dichotomy because both Paul and the evangelists want to focus on the centrality of Christ. The most creative bridge to connect letter with gospel, and both with Christ, is the concept of 'faith'.

In the gospels we see Jesus both teaching and living the nature of faith. In the letters Paul places faith as the cornerstone of individual discipleship. Without faith there is no connection with Christ; through faith we both die with Christ and live with him. 'By faith' writes Karl Barth in his magisterial *Commentary on Romans* 'the primal reality of human existence enters our horizon; by faith the incomparable step is taken; to faith no looking backwards is permitted: to faith, in the light of the absolute "Moment" and of the death of Christ, there is no supposition, but only reality.'[1]

If we had been at the Garden of Gethsemane, we would have seen Jesus, three sleeping disciples and a lot of rocks and scrubby olive trees, if we saw anything at all in the gathering gloom. But Jesus is wrapped up in prayer to an unseen Father and the scene could well be entitled 'faith'. Faith is first of all a conviction of the reality of things unseen. Christ's faith in God was given substance by his calling God 'Father'. Jesus put his faith in a God who had the qualities of a human father. In the journey towards the cross,

Jesus trusted in God who was worthy of obedience. Above all, faith was a relationship. Hearts and minds were linked in a common purpose. Jesus certainly spoke a lot about doing the Father's will and his model prayer was 'your will be done'.

Of Jesus' love and commitment and obedience to the will of the Father there is no doubt. The dilemma, on which the New Testament is built, is to what extent Jesus expected a kingdom on earth ruled by God, or a kingdom of heaven that would supersede this earthly state altogether. It is a dilemma that perplexes thinking people in the Church to this day, some working for a heaven on earth, and some preparing for a transformation of all earthly reality into the kingdom of heaven.

Jesus' faith in God seems, from the evidence, to be open to both possibilities. In that sense, his faith was unconditional. It was not prescribed by a personal agenda. God would provide and take the lead in providing. It was Jesus' duty to warn the disciples of its coming, but of the time or the date no one knew. At the end, Jesus' obedience was narrowed down to handing himself over like a child or a sick person into the will of the heavenly Father. The outcome of this obedience to death leads us into the complex area of the resurrection, in which faith played and still plays a significant role.

Abraham and 'faith'

Jesus inherited a long tradition of faithfulness to God, beginning with the faith of Abraham. Abraham is called the father of faith. He trusted in God to provide him with a family and he showed his obedience to God in being prepared to sacrifice his son Isaac. However dramatic that story is, it seems to us quite a strange outcome for faith, being asked to offer our son for sacrifice and the test being rescinded at the last possible moment. We are aware, in the case of Christ, that the history of faith was purified of earthly motive, but the seeds of trust in God were understood to have started with Abraham. The Hebrew scriptures, our Old Testament, are a history of that relationship of faith, with all its ups and downs.

Some documents are concerned with the way it progressed in history through battles, some in the development of the Temple as a focus for the worship and praise of God. Others trace the trials that challenged faith in God through exile and personal suffering, such as in the book of Job. The Psalms are an anthology of the whole spectrum of responses to God that faith evoked. Faith gave rise to joy and despair, celebration and mourning, anger and peace. Faith needed encouraging and directing.

The human side of faith is variable and in the Old Testament God too takes on a very human face, sometimes of anger and sometimes of delight. In Jeremiah, who is thought to be the author of some of the Psalms, we see the character of a Christ-like commitment to the will of God under great pressure of circumstances. From the school of Isaiah, heartfelt longings for a Messiah of God are thrown forward into the future: longings that those committed to the Isaiah tradition would not see fulfilled in their lifetime. Consequently, faith gave the Israelites a particular understanding of God which was the cause of them having to live in two worlds, the 'now' and the 'not yet'. This meant that they called on faith as a real survival strategy.

Faith seems to be a very human gift. It is the consciousness of a relationship with God, a peculiar and glorious human trait, where humanity meets God. That meeting comes often by surprise and people cannot say exactly where it comes from. One moment life is lived as best it can be and then suddenly a completely new quality comes to it. It is the same person but transfigured, as if the colour gold was flowing through the veins; joy and hope and strength even in weakness take over our lives.

An extraordinary sense of abandonment to the will of God comes upon us and 'faith' in God has meaning, although it is difficult to describe in words. Some have managed to write about the experience and none better than the seventeenth-century vicar of Credenhill, Thomas Traherne, in his poem 'The Salutation':

> From Dust I rise
> And out of Nothing now awake
> These Brighter Regions which salute mine Eys,

A Gift from God I take.
The Earth, the Seas, the Light, the Day, the Skies,
The Sun and Stars are mine; if those I prize.[2]

In the transfiguration of Christ, itself an image of the resurrection, we see this most completely. Christ's faith is completely at one with the Father's, and friends from the ancient tradition – Moses and Elijah – support Jesus on either side. Light emanates from his whole being and God acclaims Jesus by saying: 'This is my Son, the beloved, listen to him!' (Mk. 9.7).

This sort of faith and trust in God is seen most fully in Jesus Christ. Paul's mission, his driving urgency and the subject at the heart of his letters was to convey the nature of this 'faith'. It was a way of being which came from his experience of the outpouring love and forgiveness of God and which he felt he did not deserve. He could not explain it in terms of human reason and it did not come from his commitment to the Jewish laws, or his concept of God as lawgiver. Something else was needed. He found it a living, loving quality that was an unsolicited, undeserved wonder coming from the heart of existence itself. It came from God and was made known to him through Jesus Christ. So Saul's life was changed and he put his life entirely at the disposal of Jesus Christ, 'proclaiming Jesus in the synagogue, saying, "He is the Son of God" ' (Acts 9.20).

Paul, the last of the apostles

Coming to Paul after reading the gospels produces something of a literary shock for us. In the gospels we have plenty of incident, story and character. Generally the narrative moves in a linear direction, from the early days of Jesus through to the crucifixion, the resurrection and the ascension (Matthew and Luke). The gospels are as near as we can get to modern-day biography. We empathize with Jesus, feel for him, go with him along the way and relate to him as a living human being.

Christ is the inspiration for most of Paul's letters, but as an influence rather than a described reality. The human interest in the letters is largely to do with the story of Paul himself in and out of prison, his visiting of the Christian communities and in the descriptions of the attempt of those communities to live in the 'Way' that Paul was encouraging. Yet to enter fully into the spirit of Paul's letters we have to get excited about our inner motives, the drives that direct our lives and allow us to be influenced by the invisible power of God. Then we have to trust that the opening of ourselves to Christ will transform and make us fit for eternal life. It is unlikely that we shall have any desire to do so unless we have first heard about Jesus and his sacrifice for us on the cross, and so the urgency of communication is a major priority for Paul. This priority was hampered by his imprisonment but not stopped altogether, because there are the letters, the disciples, and the converts that his missionary journeys have already secured for the gospel. The journeys that Paul made are described in Luke's sequel to his gospel the Acts of the Apostles, and the letters Paul sent to newly established 'churches'. They provide a combination of theology, practical advice, hymns (Phil. 2.5–11), matters of church order and some memorable rhetorical passages in which he stretches his literary style to the greatest heights for the sake of the gospel of love. (1 Cor. 13).

We have to imagine, after the death of Jesus, that the accounts of his life and teaching were beginning to take shape in a variety of manuscripts in various places, circulating between small groups of Jews who were inspired by the memory of the resurrection. To this major religious experience were added the memories of Jesus' teaching, biographical details and accounts of miracles.

Paul, an intellectual Jew, conscious of having to write for the newly-formed congregations who followed the Way, had an impressive pedigree. Here was a zealot, and one of those committed to stamping out the Galilean sect, who came head to head with the beauty of the influence of Christ in the martyr Stephen. Paul was present at the stoning of Stephen – 'the witnesses to the stoning laid their coats at his feet' (Acts 7.58). Shortly afterwards he must have begun to sense a shift in his conscience and was becoming the good soil of the parable, ready to receive the seed of an altogether new direction in his life. This was to come in his meeting Jesus on the Damascus road.

The conversion of Paul would have taken place in the late 30s AD, when some of the earliest parts of the gospels were in the process of being written down and the later parts had not yet been devised. In forming his ideas of Jesus he would not have been working with a finished group of gospels, but from fragments and from his experience of small Christian gatherings where the Eucharist was celebrated, prayers were said and memories shared. The religious culture was fluid and many Christians still maintained a strong sense of their Jewish identity, while others began from a Gentile or pagan background.

Paul's understanding of Christ

Paul's understanding of the nature of Christ has more to do with an idea of him than the description of a personality as we might understand it. He tells us a little of what Jesus did, where he went and what he said, but Paul's central idea was that Christ (his favoured name for Jesus) was now accessible to all who bore Christ's name and someone they could mystically 'inhabit'. The notion of Christ having space within sounds strange, but was not completely foreign to the contemporary understanding of prayer, then or now. When we pray there can be a sense that our love of Christ is enabling us to grow within him. The physiological barriers to what we think and feel disappear and we can work on a model where one can inhabit another through the power of thought and feeling, will and desire. We can be 'in Christ' and Christ can dwell in our hearts in love.

So for us to be 'in' Christ, and for Christ to be 'in' us, are metaphors, ways of speaking about the unity of Christ and ourselves. However, it goes further than just a literary metaphor and represents an intimacy of being that conveys a power of love far greater than we can ever know with a human partner. The delicacy with which this picture of the indwelling of Christ had to be shared with the Church at Corinth was not lost on Paul and he was at pains to explain, as part of his sexual ethics, that such indwelling was a prerogative of Christ – the Holy Spirit – and marriage allowed an entry into that mystery, but profligacy did not. In fact profligacy literally trespassed against the Holy Spirit and was the cause of his structures against casual and 'unnatural' sex.

The idea of being 'in Christ' and Christ indwelling the individual believer was extended from a one-to-one relationship to a corporate sense of unity where all who look to Christ become a unity in the Godhead of Father, Son and Holy Spirit. The increasing sophistication of this idea, which has its very simple roots in Jesus' own experience, took several centuries to work its way through into a formal teaching on the Trinity of Persons.

There is no doubt that Paul's ideas were influenced by Greek philosophy, Jewish mystical writings and the writings of the Gnostics. No one writes without some sort of pedigree, but obviously there have been long debates through the centuries about the validity of Paul's interpretation of Christ. The simple Galilean is not so simple after all, and yet at the heart of that idea of the indwelling Christ, which some call mystical, lies the concept of 'love'.

Love (*agape*)

That humans have the capacity to feel love towards one another in the form of attraction and practical care and attentiveness, and then as self-sacrifice, are realities that draw our minds away from simple bodiliness of love into a mutuality and a sense of union one with another. This is partly physical, but much more than that, it reaches at its furthest edge into inexplicable realms of glory, peace and creativity. We call that experience love and when 'love' is no longer the word, we lapse into silence, awe, adoration and wonder. For the Christian, and for Paul, that love is intimately connected with Christ.

Why is this? For Paul it was to do with Christ being our connection with God. God the creator gave us all the resources for being who we were in the first place and Christ restored the spoilt goods of human sin and failure by his loving sacrifice on the cross. Paul gathered all that experience into his use of the word 'love'. Writing in Greek where there are at least four words for love, Paul chose *agape*, the most purged of all, which indicates the love of God. We find this comprehensively explored in his prose-poem on the theme of love in 1 Cor. 13:

> Love never ends. But as for prophecies, they will come to an end; as for tongues, they will cease; as for knowledge, it will come to an end. For we know only in part, and we prophesy only in part; but when the complete comes, the partial will come to an end. When I was a child, I spoke like a child, I thought like a child, I reasoned like a child; when I became an adult, I put an end to childish ways. For now we see in a mirror, dimly, but then we will see face to face. Now I know only in part; then I will know fully, even as I have been fully known. And now faith, hope, and love abide, these three; and the greatest of these is love.

Paul and the mind of Christ in Philippians

Embedded in the letter to the Philippians is a short poem. It is a remarkable piece of worked theology on the subject of what Christ's purpose was and how that purpose related to those who followed him then and, by implication, those who follow him now. Paul leads up to the poem with an appeal for unity among the followers of Christ, for a sense of fellow feeling, a common mind and purpose rooted in the will of God as seen in Jesus Christ.

We move from prose to poetry via a section (2.1–4) that gradually gathers momentum in a series of short requests, culminating in the most compelling and mysterious of them all: 'let the same mind be in you that was in Christ Jesus' (Phil. 2.5). The Greek has a verb 'be minded'. Some of the English translations have a noun 'let this *mind;*' others have a verb '*take to heart* among yourselves'. The difficulty about the noun 'mind' is that we immediately turn to the engine in the brain and the individual brain at that; but the Greek '*phrones*' would seem to suggest a wider, less intellectual, more general orientation of ourselves towards the work and mission of Christ. With our atomized, Western minds we have narrowed the meaning down to one isolated intellect copying another isolated intellect. It becomes a case of 'me copying Jesus, me jumping into Jesus' mind, clever me or clever Jesus, honouring clever me with his brain'.

More likely, though less romantic, is the suggestion that we think here corporately, as a body of believers, insisting on the work of Christ as a model of communal life. I say 'less romantic' because in the nineteenth century there was a growing sense of the power of the individual as creator. The isolated writer in the tower or on the lakeside communing with nature and with themselves, 'wandering lonely as clouds'. Individual genius, the 'personality' admired and adored, is a cultural influence that we have inherited in our own day. The idea of writing anonymously for the sake of a community, as our worship and liturgy have been over the centuries, runs counter to the admiration of a solitary, individual genius.

However, the New Testament encourages a similar individualism and focus on one person. We tend to see Jesus as a single romantic figure and read the New Testament as a witness to that individualism. Jesus can become for us a prototype Hamlet, a tragic hero, with a beautiful but misunderstood mind. The strange thing is that individuality does indeed remain part of the picture of Christ, because we understand individuality to be an essential part of being human. Each individual is unique, but in the light of Christ's example and teaching, the person is not alone but incorporated into God and intimately linked through Christ with all humanity. Consequently, in Paul's terms, to have the same mind as Christ Jesus is to be aware of both a divine and a human axis and both a solitary and communal identity. We see ourselves 'in Christ' not only as single isolated individuals but also as part of a whole human family past and present.

Christ, through our baptism, lowers us into death and by our faith in him raises us to eternal life. The hymn is a paradigm for 'life in Christ': *Let this mind be in you that was in Christ Jesus,*

> Who, though he was in the form of God,
> did not regard equality with God
> as something to be exploited

> but emptied himself
> taking the form of a slave,
> being born in human likeness ... (Phil. 2.6–7)

The paradox is that to love God, we have to leave God and take on the mantle of humanity, which is a lonely task at times. It is a struggle to be human; there was for Jesus, however much he turned to God for help, still this element of separation. In the mind of God, can we say, this was an essential separation in order to bring the world back to himself. Jesus was God's Son and the responsibility of the Son was to bring the world back into relationship with the Father. Paul understood it this way and embraced the mythological language in which an essential truth was being conveyed. He realized that the key to this transformation was 'faith', the faith that Jesus taught us both by word and in deed.

> Being born in human likeness ...
> And being found in human form,
> he humbled himself
> and became obedient to the point of death –
> even death on a cross. (Phil. 2.7–8)

The movement of the poem is powerful. It brings us down with Christ, physically sharing in the descent. And yet is there not, in this line, the faintest glimmer of an ascent as well? We are left at the end of the line with 'a cross' but the cross has height, verticality. The cross lifts our eyes and our hearts upward as it lifted Jesus and we prepare with him for the ascent to the Father:

> Therefore God has highly exalted him
> and gave him the name
> that is above every name,
> so that at the name of Jesus
> every knee should bend,
> in heaven on the earth and under the earth,
> and every tongue should confess
> that Jesus Christ is Lord,
> to the glory of God the Father. (Phil. 2.9–11)

It seems awkward treating Christ as a paradigm for everything we do in this life, as if every little thing has so much importance. Perhaps we don't have to personalize all this too quickly, but spend time thanking God that Christ was able to do it for us. Generally we live on a more simple domestic level making small acts of humility, which are often all too easy to achieve. It is far more useful to reflect on those who live lives of suffering love, even when everything is stacked against them. We think of mothers who have to watch their children die of AIDS or starvation, for want of water or medical resources. The notion of humbling is not glamorous. To follow Christ is to be, in any situation, open to a service that drains from us spiritual strength and empties us of it because we let it flow out to another. We do this not because we know in our mind that it is the way of Christ and therefore might reap its benefits, but because of the love of Christ which means we can do no other. The effect of our actions, and the future, are in God's hands.

Paul and the mind of Christ in 1 Corinthians 2

It has never been too difficult for me to feel comfortable with the idea of being 'in Christ', which is another of Paul's great concepts. For those with a very practical way of looking at things the concept of sharing space with another in an abstract way, being part of one another but not in a physical way, could be quite difficult. Yet we do feel with those we love and who live thousands of miles away a very special bond of love or friendship. Distance is a reality, but it does not sever all relationships. We can say that there is the telephone or video links, but even without all that there is still a sense of togetherness. We know they know we love them and they know we know they love us.

As I was growing up the feeling that I was surrounded by the love of Christ, absorbed in it, being fed by it and shaped by it was a very strong one. The medieval mystic, Mother Julian of Norwich, used physical, enfolding images for the spiritual reality of being as close to Christ as it is possible to be on this earth: 'We pray to

God because of his holy body and precious blood, his precious passion and his most dear death and wounds. As the body is clad in clothes, and the flesh in the skin, and the bones in the flesh, and the heart in the whole, so are we clothed, body and soul, in the goodness of God and *enfolded* in it.'[3]

We are enfolded in the love of Christ. We are in Christ as we shelter in his love. 'He is our clothing. In his love he wraps and holds us. He enfolds us for love, and he will never let us go.'[4]

The notion of sharing the mind of Christ is an adjunct of this incorporation into Christ. Two people can think alike, as with husband and wife. Close and intimate friends can be of like minds. So it is with Christ. There need be nothing mystical about it. If you spend part of every day in prayer with Christ then, inevitably, a relationship is made and can deepen. Christ who died and rose again to be with us forever has made himself available in a resurrected state. The physical has been absorbed into the spiritual, but not destroyed. All that the physical meant in terms of presence, identity and communication remains, but now as 'idea'. The touch is now a spiritual touch, the kiss a spiritual kiss. It is the spaces between things and the silence between words that now allow for real communication and the realm of the Spirit begins to seem more real than the material. Not more 'useful' in a practical way like a hammer to hammer in a nail, but of much greater interest, and of deeper concern. So Paul, in chapter 15 of the first letter to the Corinthians, describes a new reality in which death has been conquered by a new form of life 'in Christ', intimations of which are present in this life through faith.

Setting out on the first chapter of 1 Corinthians all things seem to be in place for Paul. All that has been described above and more is giving him a great sense of all things new. He is on fire with the sense of breaking through into a new way of relating and being which is not stuck in the limitations of the body, but feeds off this new reality of life in the Spirit. He feels it to be an interim period before the full revelation of Christ will come to complete all things.

Meanwhile, those inspired by the resurrection of Christ, the gift of the Spirit and the growth of the small Christian communities are waiting, some with impatience and some with more obvious acrimony and division. To these unsettled people Paul needs to write like an angel to give them courage, hope and joy in believing. He encourages them to realize that to follow Christ is something quite new. It is not a new sort of philosophy that they might not be clever enough to work out. On the contrary, it is in comparison a way of foolishness. It is a way that has to give up relying on human wisdom and lay itself open to the way of Christ, and that way, with its rejection of riches and its commitment to the service of Christ (Phil. 2.7), does seem like a new sort of foolishness.

The word upon which the whole system depends is the word 'spiritual'. 'Those who are unspiritual do not receive the gifts of the Spirit, for they are foolishness to them, and they are unable to understand them because they are discerned spiritually' (1 Cor. 2.14). 'Spiritual' is a much used word today. A vast literature has grown up around it. For Paul it was in essence a way of looking at things, or more passively, a way of receiving insight. The German poet Rilke called it 'inseeing', and Gerard Manley Hopkins 'inscape' or 'instress'. We have to imagine it as something that meets at the point of our receiving and Christ's giving. We have to imagine it as a gift, rather than as something we do, and many of us are not very good at receiving gifts.

Those who wait on Christ, however inadequately, are by definition 'spiritual'. They are opening themselves to the life that Christ and only Christ can give. We begin to see things through the eyes of Christ. Above all, and here Paul talks the language of the mind, we possess or have the mind of Christ. Again this close and deep relationship with Christ allows us access to his love, his thoughts, his power and ultimately his mind. We share his *phroneema* (his mind), his way of looking at things.

What a joy and relief it is, at last, to focus on one source, one fount, one conduit of inspiration for living life and a way that does open up truth of an eternal nature. The Spirit calls and we respond. The alchemy of conversion meets at this point of ultimate obedience and ultimate freedom.

We are treading on sacred ground here, because this seems to be the very centre of the matter, which is our 'incorporation' into Christ. What more could we want? But dare we ask questions even at this sacred point? For example, what has happened to the heart? Putting on the mind of Christ, have we not got too clever and lost the warmth of love that is symbolized so beautifully by the heart? To put on the mind of Christ seems cold in comparison and, awed by Paul's brilliance, we wonder whether the language of the heart has not got lost underneath a great cosmic strategy. The cup of water for the thirsty, the kissing of the leper, the kindly word at the right moment and the arm around the shoulder of those who weep and mourn are the hallmark of a pastoral ministry and a genuinely compassionate life.

When Paul talks of 'mind', he surely means more the whole movement of our being, heart, brain, soul, desire, will, memory and hopes are all held in the being of Christ. The heart is not separate from the mind, it is part of our nature orientated to the working of love, so that all is gathered into the possession of Christ, who is 'all and in all'. (Col. 3.11).

Notes

1   Karl Barth, *The Epistle to the Romans*, Edwyn Hoskyns (trans.) (Oxford: Oxford University Press, 1968), p. 201.
2   Thomas Traherne, *Poetical Works* (London: P.J. & A.E. Dobell, 1932), p. 3.
3   Julian of Norwich, *Enfolded in Love, Daily Readings* (London: Darton, Longman & Todd, 1980), p. 6.
4   Ibid., p. 1.

Chapter 5

A mind to confront

'What if it turned out that *The Brothers Karamazov* were really a religious book? And what if reading it should open up new depths in our soul and make us see everything in a new light – and perhaps realize everything is not quite so simple as devoting oneself to religious practices... but that true life is in really loving God.' *Thomas Merton*[1] 28 August 1956

Jesus and the battle of good and evil

Jesus was not by nature confrontational. Yet as a result of his mission to present the will of God to his disciples and to the people of his time, confrontation became inevitable. Various battle lines were set up. There was the line between those who lived by the letter of the religious law and those who sought to live by the love of God. Of course, in practice, there were overlaps. Jesus said, 'I have not come to abolish the law but to fulfil' (Mt. 5.17).

Goodness inevitably draws to itself the poison of wickedness and Jesus found that he became irresistibly attractive, in a paradoxical way, to those who were possessed by demons. Mary Magdalene 'of whom seven demons had gone out' could not have been more devoted to Jesus. Even now our churches attract people in all sorts of need. Holiness in some strange way attracts its opposite and the confrontations of the New Testament can be felt as powerfully today on the porches of our city churches as they were by the lakeside in Galilee in Jesus' day.

The age-old tradition of refuge, however much abused today, lingers on. The cries and taunts of the gospels ring out today, 'What have you to do with me, Jesus, Son of the Most High God?'

(Mk. 5.7). There is no reason to cease pursuing holiness just in order to avoid conflict and confrontation. Jesus went into the desert to strengthen his resolve for greater battles later on. We, like him, must put on the armour of God: 'Put on the whole armour of God, so that you may be able to stand against the wiles of the devil. For our struggle is not against enemies of blood and flesh, but against the rulers, against the authorities, against the cosmic powers of this present darkness, against the spiritual forces of evil in the heavenly places.' (Eph. 6.11–12).

One of the most persistent mythological creatures presented to us in the gospels is the devil. There is no doubt that Jesus had to consider ways of dealing with this reality. How did he picture the devil, how did he understand the workings of this character and how did he respond? The popularity of C. S. Lewis' *Screwtape Letters* has led a whole generation into assuming that the devil is a rather wily, intelligent character who was just waiting for a suitably intelligent sparring partner to defeat in debate. There is certainly something of that in the gospels with material that Matthew shares with Luke (Mt. 4.3–10; Lk. 4.1–13). Mark is, as usual, briefer, unaware of the dialogue that Matthew and Luke report. Mark tells of Jesus being driven out into the wilderness, a place open to the influences of spirits and that he was there forty days tempted by Satan. It is an unemotional little passage, which doesn't say whether Jesus was scared or what effect it had on him, nor whether it shifted his or Satan's ground. It simply says: '. . . he was in the wilderness for forty days, tempted by Satan, and he was with the wild beasts; and angels waited on him.' (Mk. 12.13).

Matthew and Luke record a combat between the devil and Jesus and it is described by means of the spareing use of Old Testament quotations. The temptation for Jesus to break his forty-day fast is countered by a verse from Deuteronomy, 'One does not live by bread alone' (Deut. 8.3; Mt. 4.4). The temptation to throw himself off the parapet of the Temple is countered by Jesus with the phrase from Deuteronomy, 'Do not put the Lord your God to the test' (Deut. 6.16; Mt. 4.7). And for a third time Jesus makes a riposte to the devil, who tempts him to bow down and worship him. Jesus again quotes Deuteronomy, 'Worship the Lord your God and serve only him' (Deut. 6.13; Mt. 4.10).

I think we can assume that this period at the beginning of Jesus' ministry and immediately after the baptism, in which the Holy Spirit filled him with eagerness and strength to begin a healing and preaching ministry, was what we might now call a 'retreat'. There are similarities. It was, for Jesus, a time free of the normal daily routine. It was a time of prayer and fasting. Long hours could be spent meditating on God and one's own life. Food if not given up altogether is plain and simple and drink is limited to water. Retreats are increasingly popular ways of coming closer to God through silence, reading, walking and worshipping, and through the spiritual guidance of a director.

Yet there were with Jesus significant differences. His was a solitary and silent retreat and although angels waited on him, Satan prodded and probed him. The gospels show us Jesus remaining firm in his faith and in his acknowledgement of the primacy of God, as understood from Deuteronomy. We don't know more than that from this particular period. However, the brief account of Jesus in the Garden of Gethsemane shortly before his crucifixion gives us another insight into the struggles that might have been part of his whole ministry. That is, the struggle of obeying the will of God and the definite desire to follow through the implications of that 'will' in practice even though it meant death.

There is a strong suggestion that Jesus lived in a world that took the presence of evil in human form quite literally. Evil incarnate could talk, tempt, goad and tease; it could wield evil influence. This is a language, a way of speaking that has come under huge scrutiny in the modern world. Whether there is a devil or not is a question that is unlikely finally to be settled. Some understand it as simply an easy way of talking about a great but palpable mystery. Yet realities of evil are all about us – cruelty, murder and rape on the individual level; terrorism and wars on an international scale. Then there are the evils of neglect, ignorance and institutional violence. The representations of evil and cruel images often reinforce ways of behaving that normally lead to more evil.

Jesus confronts those realities in his imagination and weighs them up against the good: the good that he knows exists through obedience to the reality of God. The implication of the gospels is that evil, although fully experienced by Jesus, did not damage his moral goodness, yet may well have sapped his spiritual strength. There is never the sense that Jesus is the 'iron man', but returns from the wilderness supported by the Holy Spirit and is able to meet the havoc wreaked by evil. Echoes of the Lord's Prayer – bread, evil, sins, the will of God being done – take on a rich resonance from the accounts of the time Jesus spent in the wilderness. The Lord's Prayer may well owe its provenance to those days Jesus spent in the solitude of the desert.

There has been a long spiritual tradition in the Church that follows the particular calling to the desert that Jesus underwent from time to time. Long before Jesus, Moses led his people in the wilderness and forged the commandments for them that held out the primacy of the command to love God and to love our neighbour (Lev. 19.18). Elijah came closer to God in the wilderness and formed his prophetic vocation through suffering and despair. The desert saints of the early Church, Antony of Egypt (c. 251–356), Cassian (c. 360–after 430), Paul of Thebes (died c. 340) and many others have left us nuggets of wisdom in pithy and sometimes humorous stories which lead us into the gospel ways of love and to the primacy of God.

Seraphim of Sarov (1759–1833) and desert spirituality

Seraphim of Sarov was one of those saints, perhaps closest to our own generation, who followed the path of Jesus into the desert. In Seraphim's case the desert was a forest hermitage in Russia where for sixteen years he lived as a solitary committed to prayer. It was on the name of Jesus that his prayer focused and through that name and in calling on that name for help and mercy, he found inner peace and sobriety of body and soul. At the same time, it was dynamic in its impact, becoming like a spring of living water flow-ing ceaselessly in the soul. In 1815 the time came for his cell door to be opened. It was rarely to be closed again. People flocked to him for spiritual guidance, sometimes as many as 2,000 in one day.

Seraphim's own influences included the writings of Isaac of Syria who was born in the province of Qatar, on the western shore of the Persian Gulf, sometime in the first half of the seventh cen-tury. Both Seraphim and Isaac experienced the desert as a place of battle between the Holy Spirit and the forces of darkness and evil. Indeed this was the very same battle that Jesus fought at the outset of his public ministry when he went into the desert for forty days. Isaac the Syrian wrote this on the matter of following Christ:

> Do not be astonished if, when you begin to practice virtue,
> severe tribulations break out against you on every side.
> Virtue is not accounted virtue if it is not accompanied by
> difficulty and labours. That is why all those who in the fear
> of the Lord wish to live in Jesus Christ will suffer affliction.
> For he says, 'If any want to become my followers, let them
> deny themselves and take up their cross and follow me. For
> those who want to save their life will lose it, and those who
> lose their life for my sake will find it' (Mt. 16.24–25; 10.39).
> For this reason, then, our Lord places before you the cross,
> that you might sentence yourself to death, and then send
> forth your soul to go after him.[2]

To enter the desert is to lay oneself open to the hidden forces of the universe. Even alone in one's own room, if you are lucky enough to have a space in the house which you can call your own, then if you enter into prayer and call on the name of Jesus there will inevitably be struggles of attention and of conscience. Entering into the truth of your own existence, facing the sad and unworthy things, will bring you to the heart of your need for a loving God. The desert, the cell, the quiet space, is a place where the battles of the universe are fought. God, however, provides for us 'silence and honey cakes' as Rowan Williams reminds us in his book of that name. He writes about a brother struggling with temptation who is given this advice: 'Go. Sit in your cell and give your body in pledge to the walls', and Williams understands its meaning in contemporary language as espousing reality rather than unreality, 'the actual limits of where and who you are rather than the world of magic in which anything can happen if I want it to'. He goes on,

> Is that I wonder the key to understanding the temptation of Jesus to worship Satan in exchange for 'all the kingdoms of the world'? . . . Satan wants Jesus to join him in the world where cause and effect don't matter, the world of magic; Jesus refuses, determined to stay in the desert with its hunger and boredom, to stay in the human world with its conflict and risk. He refuses to compel and manipulate people into faith because it can only be the act of a *person*, and persons do not live in the magic world. Indeed, we could well say that Jesus above all is literally 'a body pledged to the walls', to the limits of this world.[3]

The desert is a place of struggle and of vision, a place of wisdom and emptiness. And yet since it is empty there is room for the Holy Spirit to fill it with love and power, with hope and joy, and the desert feeds us with silence and honey cakes.

The Brothers Karamazov

I began to read Dostoyevsky's novel *The Brothers Karamazov* in Birmingham Public Library. A friend who was deeply immersed in the thought of the Orthodox Church suggested I read it. I was an impressionable soul and was thirsty for material that would maintain those spiritual feelings I had experienced so strongly that afternoon at the monastery. Back in the normal world of rush and the anxiety of life, this book opened up a world of spiritual wisdom. It breathed out the spirit of Russian holiness.

The character Alyosha in the book was immediately recognizable. He was searching for God, naïve and under the influence of a saintly Orthodox monk called Father Zossima. The world of holiness, wisdom, prayer, asceticism and spiritual oversight, were all roaming across the pages of this great Russian novel. This was 'desert spirituality' before I even knew the meaning of the term. The Holy Spirit was a major character both in the novel and in the haphazard circumstances of my life. Things were coming together in a miraculous way. Links were being made. God was working through the experience of the desert, even back in the 'real world'.

In the novel, Father Zossima is a spiritual father to many, but particularly to Alyosha. Alyosha comes to see Zossima at the monastery hearing that his spiritual father is near to death. Father Zossima is delighted to see him. 'Welcome my gentle one, welcome my dear boy, here you are at last I knew you'd come.'

Alyosha goes up to him, prostrates himself before him and weeps. Something surges up in his heart, his soul trembles, he feels like sobbing.[4] In fact, Zossima still has a considerable amount of strength left in him, and he appeals to Alyosha to return home to look after his brother who by some supernatural means Zossima knows was in need of help and that 'great suffering was in store for him'.

Alyosha is perplexed by what Zossima says and Zossima explains why he thinks Alyosha can help. The narrative continues with a vivid description of the relationship between the spiritual father and Alyosha and the nature of Alyosha's sanctity.

'"And you, Alyosha, I have blessed in my mind many times in my life for your face, know that," said the elder with a gentle smile. "This is what I think of you: you will go forth from these walls, but you will live in the world like a monk. You will have many adversaries, but even your enemies will love you. Life will bring many misfortunes to you, but it is in them that you will find happiness and you will bless life and make others bless it – which is what matters most."'[5]

Zossima, you could say, is a nineteenth-century desert monk living in a monastery in the woods of Russia. Dostoyevsky uses Zossima to portray the character of many holy men who set themselves apart to be available and to share the mind of Christ with thousands. The novel continues with a story within a story which begins with an account of Fr Zossima's brother who, despite his terminal illness, manages to see the world as full of life, love and hope. He shows signs of having a deeply Christian soul and says to his mother:

> 'Mother, my dearest heart, my joy, you must realise that everyone is really responsible for everyone and everything. I don't know how to explain it to you, but I feel so strongly that it hurts. And how could we have gone on living and getting angry without knowing anything about it?' So he used to get up every day, feeling more and more joyful and tender towards everyone and all vibrating with love. Zossima's brother dies and at the time, he says, it did not affect him that greatly, because he was then a very young child, 'but it left an indelible impression in my heart, a feeling that lay dormant for years. It was to come to life and respond in time. And so it happened.'[6]

This account of the faith of Zossima's brother and of his death is followed by a remarkable section entitled in Alyosha's account 'Of the Holy Writ in the Life of Father Zossima'. Zossima has kept his childlike love of the Bible.

> I had a book of Stories from the Holy Scriptures with beautiful illustrations called *One Hundred and Four Sacred Stories from the Old and New Testaments* and I learnt to read from it ... but even before I learned to read I remember how I was just moved by deep spiritual emotion when I was eight years old. My mother took me alone to church ... It was a sunny day, and I remember now, just as though I saw it again, how the incense rose from the censer and floated slowly upwards, and how through a little window from the dome above, the sunlight streamed down upon us and, riding in waves towards it, the incense seemed to dissolve in it. I looked and felt deeply moved and for the first time in my life I consciously received the first seeds of the word of God in my soul. Then a boy stepped forth into the middle of the Church carrying a big book, so big that I thought at the time

that he could hardly carry it, and he laid it on the lectern,
opened it and began to read. And it was then that I suddenly
understood for the first time, for the first time in my life,
what they read in church. 'There was a man in the land of
Uz, and that man was perfect and upright...' (Job 1.1)[7]

The desert tradition of spirituality is imbued with stories of the
wise desert fathers and mothers. Some are brief and some, as in
the case of Dostoyevsky, extending to novel length. The tradition
continues to this day and not only in Russia and the East. Wise
guides in the Christian life still make themselves available for con-
sultation, spiritual counsel and the sacrament of penance to those
seeking help.

The way of the pilgrim

Continuing within the Orthodox tradition, apart from the practice
of settling in the quiet and desert places to learn the wisdom of
Christ, there was also the way of the pilgrim. The journeys were
taken on foot and often without any real sense of direction. This
is similar to the 'peregrinations' undertaken by the saints of the
Celtic Church. It was left up to the Holy Spirit to guide the pilgrim,
though the Spirit was regularly to be found in people who advised
a good monastery to aim for! Jesus said 'I am the way' and so it
was 'on the way' that he was to be found, and his guidance was
discovered in all sorts of places and from the lips and hearts of all
sorts of people.

A classic text for such journeying is the book *The Way of the
Pilgrim*. An assistant chaplain in Petrograd, R. M. French, translated this Russian work into English in 1930. The original is an
anonymous work by a pilgrim who recounted his experiences as
he wandered from one holy place to another in Russia and Serbia
in the years before the liberation of the serfs in 1861. The pilgrim's
manuscript was discovered towards the end of the nineteenth century in the possession of one of the monks of Mount Athos by the

Abbot of St Michael's Monastery, Kazan, who made a copy and
later published it.

In 1943, the second part of this anonymous work was translated
into English with the title *The Pilgrim Continues his Way*, and this
part contains a section relevant to our theme of 'the mind of Christ'.
The subject is placed within the setting of the journey and like every
other experience in the book, wisdom is providentially discovered
and set in the narrative as if the Holy Spirit is the teacher. The
pilgrim, who had been staying in Pochaev, west of Kiev, had been
to church, and then set off on his way.

I had gone a little way along the street when I saw an open
window in one of the houses at which a man sat reading a
book. My way took me past that very window and I saw that
the man sitting there was one I had seen in church. As I went
by I took off my hat, and when he saw me he beckoned me
to come to him, and said: 'I suppose you must be a pilgrim?'
'Yes,' I answered.
He asked me in and wanted to know who I was and
where I was going. I told him all about myself and hid
nothing. He gave me some tea and began to talk to me.
'Listen my little pigeon; I should advise you to go to the
Solovetsky Monastery. There is a very secluded and peaceful
skete, a small monastic community dependent upon a large
monastery there, called *Anzersky*.'[8]

***

When I (the Pilgrim) had heard this invitation I took this
unexpected event as a sign for my journey from the Mother
of God whom I had asked to teach me the way to
blessedness. And without further thought I agreed at once.
And so we set out the next day. He read a book the whole
time, a book which never left his hand day or night; and at
times he was meditating about something. At last we came
to a halt at a certain place for dinner. He ate his food with the

book lying open in front of him and he was continually looking at it. I saw that the book was a copy of the gospels, and I said to him. 'may I venture to ask, sir, why you never allow the gospels out of your hand day or night? Why you always hold it and carry it with you?'

'Because,' he answered, 'from it and from it alone I am almost continually learning.'

'And what are you learning?' I went on.

'The Christian life, which is summed up in prayer. I consider that prayer is the most important and necessary means of salvation and the first duty of every Christian. Prayer is the first step in the devout life and also its crown, and that is why the gospel bids unceasing prayer ... Without prayer it is impossible to do any good and without the gospel you cannot learn properly about prayer. Therefore, all those who have reached salvation by way of the interior life, the holy preachers of the Word of God, as well as hermits and recluses, and indeed all God-fearing Christians, were taught by their unfailing and constant occupation with the depths of God's Word and by reading the gospel. Many of them had the gospel constantly in their hands, and in their teaching about salvation gave the advice; "Sit down in the silence of your cell and read the gospel and read it again."'[9]

I like the way the pilgrim pursues his fellow traveller with questions that many of us might like to ask for clarification ourselves, and it is also reassuring that the fellow traveller makes his answers really practical and helpful. ' "Open your gospel; look at it and make notes about what I say." And he gave me a pencil. "Be so good as to look at these notes of mine. Now," said he, "look out first of all in the gospel of St. Matthew the sixth chapter and read from the fifth to the ninth verses". You see that here we have the preparation or the introduction, teaching that not for vainglory and noisily, but in a solitary place and in quietude, we should begin our prayer" '.[10]

The connection that the fellow traveller makes between our understanding of scripture and the need for prayer is a fundamental one. Jesus describes what prayer is in the scriptures, as in the parable of the Friend at Midnight and the repeated request of the Importunate Widow (Lk. 18.1–8), illustrating his command that we should pray always and in every place and not grow discouraged. Yet there is a further aspect to this, in that as we obey Jesus' instructions to pray, so we begin to experience Christ himself within us. Our prayer brings us alongside the mind of Christ and so into the heart of God.

So the fellow traveller recommends the gospel of John which shows us 'the essential teaching about the secret interior prayer of the heart. In the first place we are shown it in the profound story of the conversation of Jesus Christ with the woman of Samaria, in which is revealed the interior worship of God *in spirit and in truth* which God desires and which is unceasing true prayer, like living water flowing into eternal life (Jn. 4.5–25)'.[11]

This is the teacher's final paragraph:

> Do you notice, after what I have now shown you, with what wisdom and how systematically the New Testament reveals the teaching of our Lord Jesus Christ on this matter which we have been tracing? In what a wonderful sequence it is put in all four evangelists? It is like this. In St Matthew we see the approach, the introduction to prayer, the actual form of prayer, conditions of it, and so on. Go farther. In St Mark we find examples. In St Luke parables. In St John the secret exercise of inward prayer, although this is also found in all four evangelists, either briefly or at length. In the Acts the practice of prayer and the results of prayer are pictured for us; in the Apostolic Epistles, and in the Apocalypse itself, many properties inseparably connected with the act of prayer. And there you have the reason that I am content with the gospels alone as my teacher in all the ways of salvation.[12]

And what of us? The search for wisdom and holiness to strengthen the soul against the forces of evil, by whichever name they go, has been a constant one in the Christian Church. Prayer and scripture have been the fundamental sources of such strength. Alongside this has been a constant reference to spiritual guides or confessors. In the ancient tradition the spiritual guide gave both counsel and forgiveness of sins in the name of the Holy Trinity, but also on a more informal basis was there to mediate the love of God and the wisdom of God in homely ways: to be a friend, to remain in touch by letter and now of course telephone and email. Letters seem to be the best way of holding a conversation from a distance, because you can be measured both in writing them and in reading them. The hand that writes leaves a style, something of themselves, bodily. C. S. Lewis' *Letters to Malcolm: Chiefly on Prayer*, *The Spiritual Letters* of Fr Congreve and Bishop Edward King's edited and abbreviated *Letters of Counsel* are all full of timeless wisdom and can usually be bought for under a £1 in the second-hand bookshops. They will help keep the devil at bay.

We started with the devil; where is the devil now, I wonder? Still around I expect, in us and encouraging us to follow the way of our worst selves. Sin begins a long way back in time and in us, and it is very invasive. We need to see it coming a long way off. I suppose we used to be able to sniff the devil. He gave us good warning, but sin is subtle and snake-like. If we can stop it before it gets into its stride then the victory may be ours. Spot the earliest signs and act then, and say 'no' then. Traditions of wisdom, novels and spiritual journeys are some of the possible alternatives to forty days in the desert that will go a long way to help us 'put on the mind of Christ'.

Notes

1   Thomas Merton, *A Search for Solitude,* Lawrence S. Cunningham (ed.) (San Francisco: Harper San Francisco, 1996), p. 75.
2   A.M. Allchin (ed.), *Heart of Compassion: Daily readings with Isaac the Syrian* (London: Darton, Longman, and Todd, 1989), p. 11.
3   Rowan Williams, *Silence and Honey Cakes* (Oxford: Lion Publishing, 2003), pp. 89, 90.

4 Fyodor Dostoyevsky, *The Brothers Karamazov* (Harmondsworth: Penguin Books, 1958), p. 333.
5 Ibid., pp. 334, 335.
6 Ibid., p. 339.
7 Ibid., p. 341.
8 R.M. French, *The Pilgrim Continues his Way* (London: SPCK, 1943), p. 53, 54.
9 Ibid., p. 54, 55.
10 Ibid., p. 57.
11 Ibid., p. 58.
12 Ibid., p. 60.

Chapter 6

A mind to imagine with

There comes a point when we have to admit ignorance over the matter of Christ's mind as a psychological entity. We have developed through huge advances in scientific research all sorts of knowledge about the brain and its effect on human behaviour. The sort of things we now know and the way we know them, and the nature of the world in which we know them, are very different from first-century Judea. In this chapter I want to use the concept of the mind of Christ to reflect on ways in which the imagination can help us see and pray and offer some very simple thoughts on the imaginative mind of Christ which could possibly transcend the differences of culture over 2,000 years and see how we share similar religious feelings and moral imperatives.

One Sunday evening in summer during the time I was vicar of a parish in northern Cumbria, various neighbouring parishes joined together for a joint Evensong. We invited a visiting preacher to take the weight off our shoulders and do the honours in the pulpit. It was an idyllic summer's evening among the northern fells, and not having to preach myself, and Monday being my day off, my senses were all open to sit back and receive.

The preacher said a simple and unforgettable truth about Jesus, something I might have picked up from Sunday school, but it came as a revelation. He was talking about how Jesus engaged people's imaginations and led them into deeper truths. He talked about the parable of the sower and how Jesus must have been aware of the way seeds were broadcast and how, because of the method of scattering seed, some would be bound to fall casually and perhaps wastefully along the footpath. Through the windows of the church I could see the hills, and thought of the Psalm which begins, 'I will lift up mine eyes unto the hills'. So simple and I had known it all my life, but that evening I was open for simple truths to come alive.

There were various ways in which Jesus' imagination was `formed. Firstly, we can see him being moved by the landscape of his home area, from the lake of Galilee and the surrounding hills to the bustling city of Jerusalem. Then he was deeply influenced by the society of his day through its ways of dealing with sickness, taxes, justice and religion, much of which provided material for his parables. Jesus would have read and heard readings of the Hebrew scriptures (our Old Testament) and these scriptures must have fed his imaginative life to such an extent that they became completely part of his mental world. The combination of all these influences, coupled with his sensitive awareness to the world around him, formed the Christ we recognize.

He began to see the world with great sympathy. It was a creation of God and although it inspired him, the created world was not the limit of his imaginative horizon. There always seemed to be something else beyond the 'here and now'. His religious education and sensibility were always challenging him to see deeper than just the surface of people's behaviour or their outward appearance: 'for he knew what was in everyone' (Jn. 2.25). He thought as God thought, not as people generally think. Now there were a thousand and one ways of understanding God in Jesus' day and the scriptures are full of debates about God. The insight of Jesus into the nature of God was formed by his relationship to God as Son to Father. That seems to have been the crucial factor. It was an intimacy of being which the emerging Church came to understand as unique and to this day remains the source of the Christian faith.

Huge edifices have been built upon this apparently simple faith and often get in the way of seeing as Christ saw the world. He loved God's creation, noticed its contours, its colours and its beauty. He saw it with the eyes of faith. He contemplated it and saw deeply into it. Our seeing, our contemplation, by sharing the mind of Christ, allows us to look on the world and see things differently. We begin to see details we might never have seen before because by putting on the mind of Christ we are absorbed into the Godhead and are able to look out on the world as Christ looked out on it.

This process of 'contemplation' is nothing new. The gospels themselves are exercises in contemplating the nature of Christ through his words and works. The evangelists were quick to pick up Christ's method. The early Church treasured these sayings and the memories and reflected on them in commentaries, sermons, prayers and hymns, as have writers and theologians in every century since, and not always with equanimity.

So, jumping forward a few centuries, when in the sixteenth century Ignatius of Loyola had time on his hands when a battle wound forced him to rest, he too had time to contemplate the details of the life of Christ and what they meant to him. He popularized a method of 'seeing' into the life of Christ, which has never ceased to encourage people to use their minds to imagine the depth of the love of God in the life and ministry of Jesus Christ. They have become known as *The Spiritual Exercises*.

The Spiritual Exercises of St Ignatius Loyola

One of the most discussed and popularized methods of spiritual formation over the past twenty years has been through the rediscovery of *The Spiritual Exercises of Ignatius Loyola*. The exercises, though, have been popular ever since their inception in the 1520s. Ignatius of Loyola (1491–1556) was born of a noble family at the castle of Loyola, not far south of the Pyrenees. He spent his formative years (c. 1506–17) in the household of Juan Velásquez de Cuéllar, the Royal Treasurer of Castile, and then embarked on a military career rather similar to Francis of Assisi three centuries earlier and St Martin of Tours before that. A wound in the right leg, which Ignatius received during the siege of Pamplona (1521), reduced him to a prolonged state of inactivity, during which he read among other things Ludolf of Saxony's *Vita Christi*. This caused him to change his life radically.

After his recovery Ignatius went to Montserrat where he made a general confession, hung up his sword at the altar of the Blessed Virgin Mary and exchanged clothes with a beggar. He then went to Manresa for a year (1522–3). Here he underwent a series of profound spiritual experiences from which he derived many of the insights contained in *The Spiritual Exercises*. It is the *Exercises* which contain his meditations on the life of Christ and his programme for pursuing a course of reflection on aspects of the life of Christ, which are close to our theme here.

Ignatius' pilgrim spirit had been strengthened at Manresa, when 'God treated him as a schoolmaster treats a child' and he could bear to face, with no help from image or imagination, the ascent to the solitude of God. This took place in September 1523 on one of his silent walks along the banks of the Cardoner, near the cross Del Tort high above the hermitage of St Paul. A description survives of his inmost thoughts.

When he had walked a portion of the way, he sat down and gazed at the river. The eyes of his spirit began to open. It was not that he actually beheld some vision but rather there was given to him a knowledge and understanding of many things of the spiritual life, of faith and theology. This was accompanied by a brilliant enlightenment so that everything appeared new. It was impossible to describe in detail what he then grasped. This alone can be said, that he acquired a wonderful clarity in his mind. Were he to put together all the graces of God received throughout his more than two and sixty years and add to this total all he had ever known, it would not in his judgement be as great as what he experienced on that single occasion. This experience made so profound an impression on him that his spirit remained illuminated. It was as though he was transformed into another person. He threw himself down on his knees before a crucifix which stood nearby to express his gratitude to God.[1]

The Spiritual Exercises, substantially completed by 1541, provide for a structured, individually guided programme of mainly imaginative prayer, lasting in its full form for about a month. The first week is devoted to reflection on sin and its consequences. The second week focuses on the life of Christ beginning with consideration of the kingdom and focusing on 'Two Standards' (Christ's and Satan's, 'standard' being understood in a military sense). The third week concentrates on the passion and the fourth on the resurrection. Ignatius requires the one directing the use of the exercises for others always to be sensitive, adapting the instructions to the circumstances of the individual.

The remarkable quality of the exercises resides mainly in the way in which the imagination is brought to bear on the consideration of aspects of the life of Christ. For example, when contemplating the nativity, the one undergoing the exercises would be invited to see, hear, taste and touch aspects of the scene: for example, '4. Kiss respectfully the walls of the stable, the straw in the manger, the swaddling clothes, the sacred hands and feet of Jesus.'[2] The imaginative aspect of these exercises brings us very close to the way a poet might work. Thomas Hardy uses the same technique at the beginning of his Christmas poem, 'The Oxen':

> Christmas Eve and twelve of the clock.
> 'Now they are all on their knees,'
> An elder said as we sat in a flock
> By the embers in hearthside ease.

> We *pictured* the meek mild creatures where
> They dwelt in their strawy pen,
> Nor did it occur to one of us there
> To doubt they were kneeling then.[3]

In poetry the poet creates the scene he wants others to enter into. That scene may be a physical, visual one, but it can also be an emotional one, or an exploration of an idea. Whatever the subject, it has to be 'made' by the writer to be communicated to the reader or listener. So with the *Exercises*, hints are given as to the things one might think about, or experiment with, to bring history into the present.

So, for example, Ignatius is eager to represent 'the poverty of the birth of Jesus Christ' and so he paints a picture in words to allow the reader to enter imaginatively into the scene as if they were there. St Francis, in his day, had similar thoughts and created the first crib as an aid to an imaginative involvement with the life of Christ.

1. Christ is born in a strange country, out of his mother's house, where he would have found what is never wanting even to the most neglected of poor children, a roof to shelter him and a cradle to rest in.
2. His cradle is a little straw in a manger, so that his birth resembles that of the lowest animals. He is reduced to such misery that he can say with truth even now, 'Foxes have holes and the birds of the air have nests; but the Son of Man has nowhere to lay his head.' (Lk. 9.58)
3. Every thing around him participates in his poverty; – his parents, who scarcely possess a few coarse garments to clothe him with; the poor shepherds, who at the voice of the angels leave their flocks to come and adore him.[4]

***

The Spiritual Exercises have largely been the preserve of the Society of Jesus, the Jesuits, although in the twentieth century they have been more widely used by the Church in general. The names of Hans Urs von Balthasar and Gerard Hughes, the author of the book *God of Surprises*, come to mind, but it is to Gerard Manley Hopkins that I want to turn for a deeper look at the effect of the *Exercises* on the mind of a poet. Through the eyes of Hopkins we see how the method of entering into the life and purposes of Christ, which Ignatius made famous, becomes a model for understanding the relation between the mind of Christ and the notion of the Trinity.

When we consider the mind of someone, we tend to think of their conscious mind, the decisions they make, their thoughts and actions, their likes and dislikes, what we understand of them from their birth to their death, and nothing more. With Jesus we are dealing with someone whose nature or reality stretches much further than his earthly existence. In all the gospels there is some suggestion of a preparation for the coming of Christ, a reality before the birth and a lively sense of an existence after death. Our present-day thinking does not allow for very much use of the mind other than in our worldly life. With Jesus things are different. He was in the mind of God from the beginning and exists now and will be with us to the end of time. The way Hopkins reads *The Spiritual Exercises* stretches our understanding of the mind of Christ.

Gerard Manley Hopkins (1844–1899) and *The Spiritual Exercises*

Hopkins (1844–1899) was born into an Anglican home, attended school at Highgate and went from there to Balliol College, Oxford. It was while he was at Oxford that he came under the spell of John Henry Newman and much to the horror of his family and some of his friends he was received into the Roman Catholic Church in October 1866. In the following year he took a First in 'Greats' and was proclaimed 'the star of Balliol'. For a few months after leaving the university he taught at Newman's Oratory School at Edgbaston; then in 1868, after a holiday in Switzerland, he entered the novitiate of the Society of Jesus.

On becoming a Jesuit he burnt all his poems, feeling they were not suitable for his new life unless he was invited to write by his superiors. However, his deeply poetic and artistic temperament, allied to a fervent religious faith, led him back to poetry and for that he is now best known. During the course of his life as a Jesuit he undertook *The Spiritual Exercises* on two occasions. Since each one took a month of intense prayer, meditation and self-examination, these two occasions were highly significant in his life.

The almost military discipline of the Society of Jesus is based on *The Spiritual Exercises* and the religious character of Hopkins was so effectually moulded by this discipline that many of his poems contain poetic interpretations or embodiments of the Ignatian teaching. The first time he followed the *Exercises* shortly after he entered the novitiate provided the inspiration for the writing of his great poem 'The Wreck of the *Deutschland'*. In a passage reflecting on some of the first words of the *Exercises*, 'Man was created for a certain end', Hopkins contemplates what it is to be a self made by God:

> For human nature, being more highly pitched, selved, and
> distinctive than anything in the world, can have been
> developed, evolved, condensed, from the vastness of the
> world not anyhow or by the working of common powers but
> only by one of finer or higher pitch and determination than
> itself ... And this is much more true when we consider the
> mind; when I consider my selfbeing, my consciousness and
> feeling of myself, that taste of myself, of *I* and *me* above and
> in all things, which is more distinctive than the taste of ale or
> alum, more distinctive than the smell of walnutleaf or
> camphor, and is incommunicable by any means to another
> man (as when I was a child I used to ask myself: What must
> it be to be someone else?).[5]

For Hopkins the awe with which he greeted his own humanity, was a reflection of the glory which came from Christ, the incarnate one.

Christ who was the word made flesh is also the Son of God who now draws us to his Father:

> I am all at once what Christ is, since he was what I am, and
> This Jack, joke, poor potsherd, patch, matchwood, immortal
>   diamond,
>   Is immortal diamond.[6]

(from 'That Nature is a Heraclitean Fire and of the comfort of the Resurrection')

And so we move with Hopkins in his thought to the incarnation, the earthly life of Jesus, as the image of the creator God. Hopkins finds language to unite opposites, human and divine, and so be eloquent over the great miracle of the divine coming into the human sphere so that the human can be graced with the divine. On the moral plane, especially for the Jesuit, there is always this orientation towards his highest spiritual good, which is found in Christ:

'There's none but Christ can stead you. Christ is truth.'[7]

The *Exercises* are spread over four weeks and Hopkins' *Commentary* makes a fascinating footnote both to the *Exercises* themselves and also to his poems. His direct notations to the experiential *Exercises* are perhaps the most accessible. For example, he annotates the material surrounding the birth of Jesus. (The material in italics is taken from the edition of the *Exercises* that Hopkins was using during his retreat, and his own comments on the *Exercises* follow):

Ignatius wrote '*The first point is to see the persons with the eye of the imagination, meditating and contemplating in particular on their circumstances, and from the seeing of them to get some fruit.*' Hopkins comments, 'inferring what they must have been, observing what they are'. Hopkins then continues with a passage on Mary's thoughts at the Annunciation: 'What does God ask me to do . . . how is the seed to be sown?'

'*Secondly*', Ignatius continued, '*to hear with my hearing what they say, or might say, and by reflecting on myself to get some fruit. Thirdly, to savour and to taste, by smell and by taste, the infinite delicacy and sweetness of the divinity, of the soul and of the virtues and of the rest of the things that belong to the person who I am contemplating, and by reflecting on myself to draw hence some fruit*'. Hopkins annotates, 'Smelling – here he speaks of metaphorical taste and smell. You may suppose each virtue to have its own sweetness – one rich, another fresh, a third cordial, like incense, violets, or sweet herbs, or, for taste, like honey, fruit, or wine'.

'*Fourthly*', Ignatius writes '*to touch by touching, that is to say to kiss and to embrace the ground where such persons leave their footprints; and the place where they recline, always with a view to the fruit that I may draw from thence*'. Finally, Hopkins comments, '"Touching" etc – I suppose St Ignatius means us to do what we might have done if present and not to do what we should not have ventured to have done, and this shows how strongly he means us to realise the scene.'[8]

It is fascinating to see how Hopkins' mind is working on the *Exercises*. We see him thinking through his own celibacy as he reflects on birth and Mary's virginity. We notice his relish of the senses as a means to greater understanding of the nature of Christ's humanity. In addition we see how his poetry was influenced by the Ignatian method of contemplation: 'the hearing, seeing, tasting, touching' of realities that often evoke deeper meanings.

The religious Hopkins had a particular interest in the section in the *Exercises* concerning 'The Hidden Life'. This is his diary entry for 19 November 1881. We notice how he found Christ's hidden life up to the age of thirty a great support for his own monastic life.

The Hidden Life

The Life of Christ our Lord from the Twelfth to the Thirteenth Year 'De Vita' Nov.19.1881 (Long Retreat) – Fr. Whitty (Robert Whitty (1817–95) (An Irishman of great but very simple wisdom and holiness made a deep impression on GMH) gave last night the following pregnant thoughts:
1. He (Jesus) was obedient to them: the hidden life at Nazareth is the great help to faith for us who must live a more or less obscure, constrained and unsuccessful life. What of all possible ways of spending 30 years could have seemed so ineffective as this? What might not Christ have done at Rome or Athens, Antioch or Alexandria! And sacrificing, as he did, all to obedience his very obedience was

unknown. Repulsiveness of the place: a traveller told him, who had been twice to Nazareth, that even now it keeps its fame for rudeness and worthlessness. But the pleasingness of Christ's life there in God's eyes is recorded in the words spoken when he had just left it: 'This is my beloved son' etc. 2. What was his life there? – one of devotion, saying or singing the Psalms of David, which St Jerome used still to hear in the fields of Palestine. Also one of labour, and of obedience; in every way it looked ordinary, presented nothing that could attract the world, not even austerities like those of St John in the wilderness.
3. Our Lady's life at the same time – she was watching all he did. Twice St Luke tells us 'she laid up all these things in her heart' which therefore is a sort of fifth gospel ... and to it we must apply to know what Christ there was.[9]

***

It is not surprising that a poet-priest responded so eagerly to the method of Ignatius. The exercises have all the ingredients that were needed to provoke Hopkins into writing poetry, and not only poetry but also reflective prose. In his commentary on the *Exercises*, written during his forty-day retreat in 1881–2 at Manresa House in Roehampton, he made extensive notes and comments on the experience. Hopkins was swept up into a reflection on Christ as one who came down from and then went back up again to God. He took as his inspiration the passage in Paul's letter to the Philippians (2.7–8) '(Christ Jesus) emptied himself, taking the form of a slave, being born in human likeness. And being found in human form, he humbled himself and became obedient to the point of death – even death on a cross.'

Dealing as we are here with 'the mind of Christ', it seems reasonably straightforward if we are only using the knowledge we have of his living an essentially human life as we all do. The difficulty comes when we have to deal with Jesus before he was born and after he died. That is a problem for all of us, but with Jesus especially, because the claims concerning his life prior to birth and beyond death are so exceptional. In John's gospel the prologue (1.1–18) in particular sets out the relationship of the Word both to God and to the Word's incarnation in the flesh. Jesus, as the Word, has an existence which extends across temporal existence and beyond. 'Before Abraham was I am' could be considered quite recent history compared with 'in the beginning was the Word', and at the other end, 'I will be with you to the end of time.'

In none of the books of the New Testament are we allowed to feel that Jesus is limited to our present understanding of time and space. Always he is related in some way with God; it is that which made him unique. To talk of his mind and of the idea of sharing his mind, putting it on, having the same mindset as Jesus, hardly takes into consideration that Jesus' mind, his intentions, knowledge, scope, imaginative world, his very being, were intimately governed by the one who is the centre of all that is, which is God:

> Thou mastering me
> God! giver of breath and bread;
> World's strand, sway of the sea;
> Lord of living and dead;[10]

By limiting our concept of the mind of Christ to a brain, however ingenious, we narrow the possibilities and diminish the evidence that Christ's mind was in some way inseparable from the intentions of God. 'What God was the word' was. The meditations of the second week of the *Exercises* draws us into a concept of the Godhead that takes seriously the breadth of vision we can have in understanding God. The picture is of God in Trinity 'the three divine persons were looking at the great plain of the whole world and the circuit of it full of men'. Hopkins likes the idea of the world set out as a great plain, in which humanity is seen by the divine mind from the beginning to the end of time. It is rather reminiscent of the opening of the vision of Piers the Plowman when from the height of the Malvern hills he looks down and sees 'a faire felde ful of folke . . . of alle maner of men'. In more contemporary mode it is also reminiscent of Anthony Gormley's *Field*, with its hundreds of terracotta figures. Hopkins continues the story of how:

> It is decreed by the most Holy Trinity *in its eternity* that the Second Person *become man* to save the human race, and thus, when the fullness of time is to come, They sent the Angel St Gabriel to our lady.
>
> Second, the composition, by seeing the place. Here it will be to see *the great capacity of the world*, where there dwell so many and such diverse peoples. And thereafter to see the house and the room of Our Lady, in the township of Nazareth in the province of Galilee...
>
> The first point is to see the persons, one after the other, and first those who are scattered over the face of the earth in such great diversity...
>
> Secondly, to see and consider the three Divine Persons, as it were upon their royal throne...
>
> Thirdly, to see Our Lady and the Angel ... the Angel confirms what he said to Our Lady by announcing the conception of St John the Baptist...[11]

These very brief passages in the form of notes are a very small part of Hopkins' reflections on scripture as part of his involvement with the Ignatian exercises. The words in italics are commented on further in the text. These notes are a really fascinating insight into an area of Hopkins' thought that is not often written about. Watching a rich and fertile imagination working on scripture from a poetic and theological standpoint is a rare treat.

Extending our understanding of the mind of Christ beyond the realm of our own experience and beyond modern concepts of what is feasible is always very difficult. It is not difficult to be imaginative and to approve of scenarios which work as metaphors of transcendence, but to hold onto them as realities and still use the word in the way we use 'real' today, is to risk absurdity. This is nothing new. People have been struggling for centuries with the problem of seeing anything in the world other than what they can scientifically verify. To make sense of the prologue to St John's gospel with a one-dimensional mindset is impossible and that means we inevitably narrow down the 'mind of Christ' to what we know about minds. It would not be impossible to look at things the other way around and say 'can we allow the mind of Christ, with its roots in the mind of God, to teach us more about what *we* can be'.

Notes

1 Leonard Von Matt and Hugo Rahner, *St Ignatius of Loyola* (London: Longmans, Green & Company, 1956), pp. 34, 35.

2 *Manresa or, The Spiritual Exercises of St Ignatius* (London: Burns & Oates, undated), p. 149.

3 Thomas Hardy, 'The Oxen', in *The Complete Poems* (London: Macmillan, 1976), p. 403.

4 *Manresa*, op. cit., p. 143.

5 *The Sermons and Devotional Writings of Gerard Manley Hopkins*, Christopher Devlin (ed.) (Oxford: Oxford University Press, 1959), p. 123.

6 *The Poetical Works of Gerard Manley Hopkins*, Norman Mackenzie (ed.) (Oxford: Oxford University Press, 1990), p. 198 (from 'That Nature is a Heraclitean Fire and of the Comfort of the Resurrection').

7 Ibid., p. 83 (from 'On the Portrait of Two Beautiful People').

8 *The Sermons*, op. cit., pp. 175, 176.

9 *The Sermons*, op. cit., p. 176.

10 *The Poetical Works*, op. cit., first stanza, p. 119.

11 *The Sermons*, op. cit., p. 169.

Chapter 7

A mind to pray

'Yes, Jesus is enough for us. Where he is nothing is lacking.'
Charles de Foucauld[1]

To know how a person prays is one way to know their mind. Prayer is both a public and a private matter. The public aspect of prayer we often call worship and here the prayers are mainly set down and have a long tradition of use behind them. The private aspect of prayer is something that exists between a person and God. Private prayer is the root of a spiritual life.

Jesus' public prayer would have consisted of the prayers of the synagogue in which the Psalms played a major part. The Psalms are poetic verses that express the whole range of religious emotion from praise to despair, joy to sorrow, grievance to exaltation and include remembrance of the great acts of God from the past, and hopes for the years to come. Steeped in the Psalms, Jesus would have fashioned his mind from that source and it is recorded most famously that he cried out from the cross, 'My God, my God, why have you forsaken me?' (Ps. 22.1).

The Hebrew scriptures that Jesus heard read and later read publicly himself in the synagogue at Nazareth would have been well known to him. The various key texts recur, such as those from Isaiah telling of God's servant who suffers, and from Jeremiah criticizing the worldliness of the Temple. The mysterious writings of Daniel and Ezekiel gave Jesus the figure of the Son of Man as an image that he took to himself. In this way Jesus successfully avoided claims of being God. At the same time it enabled him to come alongside God in the role of the representative human being, who would sit at God's right hand on the day of judgement (Mk. 14.62).

What then of Jesus' private prayer? Where do we get glimpses of this in the gospels and what was the nature of that prayer? Being essentially out of the public gaze it is difficult to know except from within our own experience of prayer. Yet there are references to this important area of Jesus' life and they fall under three headings: prayer as restoration of the spirit; prayer as a gathering of strength; and prayer as a preparation to act.

Prayer as a restoration of the spirit

'In the morning, while it was still very dark, he got up and went out to a deserted place, and there he prayed' (Mk. 1.35).

'After saying farewell to the disciples, he went up the mountain to pray' (Mk. 6.46).

The internal, secret, private prayer of Jesus is by its very nature hard to enter into. The fact that Jesus sought out remote places such as hills and the desert in which to pray indicates that he needed space and quiet to listen to his own internal needs and to hear the voice of God. It was in laying himself open to the presence of God in prayer through the Holy Spirit that he came to perceive God as 'Abba' or Father. The word Abba is the original Aramaic word that Jesus would have used. It suggests that he understood God as the one who hears prayer and was a familiar, loving and accessible person, hearing in the same way as a human parent hears, takes note and listens caringly to requests for help.

Did Jesus assume, then, that God was someone who could hear with a physical human ear? Or, like us, did he use human language knowing that in the end it was a flawed means of addressing the supreme being? Did he share our anxiety over the gap between human language and divine essence, between human talk and God's creative silence? These are some of the areas it would have been helpful to talk to him about, but it is more than likely that Jesus used silence to enter into the loving silence of God.

When I visited the western side of Lake Galilee, staying near Gadara, I got up early and climbed behind the hotel to a height where I could see only the lake and lost sight of buildings. It was good to be up among the empty and silent hills and it felt very much like the homely surroundings of Grasmere Vale. It was even more compelling being in a place I had always imagined but never seen and it seemed a huge privilege to share just briefly that land-scape with one who had been the silent companion of my life all along. It was on that hill that I knew I could share a love of solitude with him.

In some ways it was no different from any place of solitude, sur-rounded by natural beauty and providing an ideal environment for quiet contemplation and just plain resting in the presence of God. Surely Jesus would have spent many hours receiving pas-sively the strength that comes from offering the empty self to God. Then, just the same as the early morning I was there, hearing the growing sound of birdsong, the rustle of small creatures and see-ing the shape of a flower or of a bush that could provide a focus for wonder and sheer thankfulness. All this I felt as the light began to rise above the hills behind me.

Prayer as a gathering of strength

'So I tell you, whatever you ask for in prayer, believe that you have received it, and it will be yours' (Mk. 11.24).

'Whenever you stand praying, forgive, if you have anything against anyone; so that your Father in heaven may also forgive you your trespasses' (Mk. 11.25).

Prayer was also a time of gathering spiritual strength and purity with which to go out and heal the sick and cast out demons. Prayer, for Jesus, often went with fasting. That helped him draw on the invisible resources of God and to find power to transform the situations that spoke of death into the possibility of hope and new beginnings. He prayed in order to have the capacity to heal, restore, cast out evil, bring calm and engender faith out of despair and unbelief. This was done, not by being a superstar, but by channelling the power of God, creator of all that is, into that place in need of healing, restoration and calm.

Prayer as a preparation for action

' "Abba, Father, for you all things are possible; remove this cup from me; yet, not what I want, but what you want" ' (Mk. 14.36).

With learning by memory and holding things longer in the memory than we do now, Jesus was able to recall the priorities of scripture, the images of the tradition and to set his own life alongside them. His prayer would have included an opportunity to make decisions on the future and to harness strength to put God's will before his own. It was in those times of prayer that his mind was made up to move towards his death. In his silent and hidden prayer he gathered the spiritual strength to go the way of the cross, rather than the way of escape and concealment. He talked to his disciples of the necessity to die so that something much more significant could be born.

This makes prayer far more than a 'saying' of prayers, or even of silent meditation. It makes it the engine of a loving commitment to a way that leads to confrontation, public acrimony, being betrayed – that is, being the one who is vulnerable, pushed around and despised. In those times with God, prayer becomes the distillation of priorities.

Both in hindsight and, we presume, at the time, an element of 'power' or 'drive' was part of this prayer. This could be just hindsight as we talk now of the Holy Spirit being the 'go-between' linking the will of the Father and the obedience of the Son, but how does it show itself now, and is that a help? Prayer is a time to encourage inspiration. Connections are made at deep levels and then become clear to us as we receive them, through prayer, into our minds. Yeats' 'rag and bone shop of the heart'[2] receives all the stuff of life and in the light of God comes into an order, a priority, and the decision is made. After three hours of prayer in the garden of Gethsemane, Jesus said, 'Get up, let us be going'. (Mk. 14.42), as if that process had reached a conclusion, provided an answer and come to the 'hour' of decisive action. Prayer had done its work.

Charles de Foucauld and the mind to pray

It has been an extraordinarily strong compulsion in some to foster closeness to Christ by praying and meditating in the actual places he lived, taught, loved, died and rose again. This is not at all surprising. The pilgrimage tradition of travelling to the Holy Land, books on the holy places and the flora and fauna of the landscape, all bear witness to the passion that these scenes have evoked. For some it has been the mainspring of their whole spiritual orientation. Charles de Foucauld (1858–1916) was just such a one.

Before any dates and list of pedigree come tumbling out let me set before you two photographs. The first is of Charles as a 'lieutenant de hussards' taken in 1880. His face looks vacant. His trim moustache is slightly curled round his sullen and sensual mouth. His hair, smoothed down, also sports a studied curl. His military clothing seems very fashionable. The second photograph was taken in 1914 when, now as Fr Charles, he is living in a simple hermitage at Tamanrasset in the middle of the Sahara desert. He spends his days kneeling before the Blessed Sacrament and providing open hospitality to the people who pass his way. His inspiration is above all the hidden life of Jesus at Nazareth. In the photograph his face is radiant, sculpted by a life of prayer and the words beneath the photograph read, 'The likeness is the measure of the love'.[3]

Ironically, his first experience of Africa was as a soldier. His regiment were sent to Algeria, but his life with a mistress produced scandal and he was sent home on temporary leave. However, on hearing that the regiment was involved in an insurrection at Bu-Aanama in South Oranais his residual sense of honour moved him to return. The thought of sacrifice had come home to his soul. The tribespeople of the Sahara made a deep impression on him and when the insurrection was over, he asked for leave in order to go on a journey in the south to study their lives. As he could not get this leave, he tendered his resignation and settled in Algiers to prepare for his great journey to Morocco.

It was in 1888, when he was thirty, that he made a significant confession of his sins and received Holy Communion from the hands of the Abbé Huvelin. Abbé Huvelin was parish priest of the church of St Augustin in Paris. Outwardly undistinguished, his influence on the spiritual lives of many Catholics at the end of the nineteenth century, including Baron von Hügel and, through von Hügel, Evelyn Underhill, was widespread. It was as a result of this act of confession that de Foucauld wrote, 'I had believed there was a God, I now understand that I can do no other than live for Him. My religious vocation dates from the same hour as my faith. God is so great. There is such a difference between God and all that is not Him'.

In that same year and until February 1889 Charles was to make his first visit to the Holy Land. In that short visit were sown the seeds of his vivid and imaginative devotion to Christ. As he wrote 'You see, it is not so difficult to love Jesus and to imitate him.' After his first brief visit to the Holy Land, he returned to France and became a Trappist monk at Notre-Dame-des-Neiges, on the high plateaux of the Vivarais. Seven years later he realized that he had to pursue a more intense and hidden form of monastic life than could be provided in the monastery, and Abbé Huvelin wrote advising him against another Trappe

> where I should prefer to see you nevertheless. The same thought will come to you there, the same comparison between the life you see and the life you follow after. *I prefer Capharnaum or Nazareth*, or some such Franciscan convent; not in the convent, but only under the shadow of the convent; asking only for spiritual assistance, living in poverty at the gate. Do not think of banding any souls around you, nor, above all, of giving them a rule. Live your life,

then; if any souls come, live the same life together without making any regulations. On this point I am quite clear.[4]

Charles did indeed find accommodation in a woodshed in the garden of the Poor Clares' convent at Nazareth. He wrote to his cousin shortly after arriving

I am settled in Nazareth; there you may henceforth write to the following address: Charles de Foucauld, Nazareth, Holy Land, *poste restante*. The good God has let me find here, to the fullest extent, what I wanted: poverty, solitude, abjection, very humble work, complete obscurity, as perfect an imitation as possible of the life our Lord Jesus in this same Nazareth. Love imitates, love wants to conform with its beloved; it tends to unite everything, their souls in the same feelings, all the moments of existence in a kind of identity of life; that is why I am here.[5]

The experience of being as close as possible, both physically and spiritually, to the hidden years of Jesus' preparation for ministry was what he desired. It was a humble and costly choice but it brought him great joy, fulfilment and happiness. It was what he felt God wanted him to do and it gave him time and the peace to pray. The stories about him are occasionally very humorous. His clothing was bizarre. He wore a long hooded blouse with white and blue stripes, blue cotton trousers and on his head a very thick white woollen cap, around which he had rolled a strip of fabric in the form of a turban. He had only sandals on his feet. A rosary of big beads hung from the leather girdle that tightened his tunic. René Bazin, his biographer, explains this in a helpful way: 'In adopting this dress, no doubt the solitary meant to expiate the smartness of former days, and to excite to some extent the scorn of the passers-by and the mockery of the children in the street, and to take all this gladly. He knew the saying of Ignatius, used by so many saints of all ages: "I prefer to be regarded as a nobody and a madman for Christ, who was thus looked upon before me."'[6]

Inspired by being in the very places where Christ lived and travelled, prayed and kept silent and grew in his love for the Father, Charles de Foucauld prayed too. He spent long hours in prayer and wrote down his thoughts in the form of prayerful meditations. They have a wonderful, childlike simplicity as we overhear him kneeling before the Blessed Sacrament, speaking directly to Jesus. Here are three examples.

'The mind of God'

I must try to know you my God, so that I may love you better; the more I know you the more I shall love you, because in you all is perfect, lovable and admirable. To know you even a little better is to behold a more radiant, a more transparent beauty, to be transported out of myself by love. In you are all my thoughts, words and actions, my God. Your own Spirit is ever brooding. Your thoughts vary not. You contemplate yourself, for you are Intellect. You love yourself, for you are Will – you love yourself infinitely of necessity, for you are Justice, and being Just, you love your own infinitely lovable and perfect Being. My God, you are in me, around me, my saviour Jesus, my God, near me in the Host, and your thoughts are *Contemplation* and *Love*.[7]

'The hidden life of Jesus'

My Jesus, who art present near me, shew me what to think about your hidden life.'He went down with them and went to Nazareth and was subject unto them.' He went down, lowered himself, humbled himself. It was a life of *humility*. My God, you appear in the likeness of man, and becoming man you make yourself the lowest of men. Yours was a life of *abjection*. You took the lowest of the low places. You went down *with them*, to live their life, the life of the poor working people, living by their labour. Your life, like theirs, was poor, laborious, hard working. They were humble and obscure. You lived in the shade of their obscurity. You went to Nazareth, a little village, lost, hidden in the mountains whence, it was said 'no good thing came forth.' It was like a retreat. You were apart from the world and the towns, in this *retreat* you lived.[8]

'The public life of Jesus'

What then, my Lord Jesus, was your public life?
    I tried to save men by word and by works of mercy. Before, in my life at Nazareth, I was content to save them by prayer and penitence. Now I show my zeal for souls publicly. But though my life became more active it was always partly solitary and was always a life of prayer and penance and interior recollection ... It was a life of fatigue, long journeys, long sermons, and days in the desert without shelter or shade cannot be without fatigue and physical suffering, intemperate weather, nights without shelter, uncertain nourishment snatched when work permitted; all these mean suffering. Then there was *moral* suffering: men's ingratitude, their deaf ears, their ill will, their hard hearts, my healing hand laid daily on all sorts of suffering of the human body. Souls saved, so many lost to be found, such human suffering, that of the righteous, that of my Mother, the vision ever growing nearer and greater of my Passion; of enmities as the only response to my words of salvation, to my words of love offered to all men; above all, the ingratitude of that 'faithless and perverse generation' wounding my tender compassionate Heart.[9]

As he pursued his vocation in Nazareth and in Ephraim and Jerusalem, Charles began to write a Rule for the new community of 'Little Brothers', hoping that others would join him and received permission to pursue this vocation. After ordination in 1901 he built a hermitage at Beni-Abbes on the border of Morocco and in 1905 moved to Tamanrasset deeper in Algeria. He lived an apostolate of 'kindness and friendship', welcoming all, 'good or bad, friend or enemy, Muslim or Christian'. Although no one then joined him, he did succeed in founding an association of lay people committed to a similar evangelical Christian lifestyle. On December 1916, he was killed at Tamanrasset by robbers. Among the thoughts contained in his final letters are these: 'This holy time of Advent, which is always sweet to me, is particularly so here. Tamanrasset, with its forty little homes of poor labourers, is just what Nazareth and Bethlehem might have been in Our Lord's day.'[10]

Lose my Life in God. The most perfect way. I should carry on in myself the life of Jesus: think his thoughts, repeat his words, his actions. May it be he that lives in me. I must be the image of our Lord in his hidden life: I must proclaim, by my life, the gospel from the roof-tops. *Veni.* My courage must be equal to my will. 'Seek thyself in me. Seek me in thyself.' 'It is time to love God.' Seek God only. Kindness. Gentleness. Sweetness. Courage. Humility. [11]

***

Notes

1 *Meditations of a Hermit, The Spiritual Writings of Charles de Foucauld,* Charlotte Balfour (trans.) (London: Burns & Oates, 1930), p. 182.

2 W.B. Yeats, 'The Circus Animals Desertion', section 3, line 8, in *Collected Poems* (London: Macmillan, 1967), p. 392.

3 Saying of Charles de Foucauld, quoted in French, 'La resemblance est la mesure de l'amour' [The likeness is the measure of the love] in Denise and Robert Barrat, *Charles de Foucauld et la fraternite, 'Maîtres Spirituels'* (Paris: Editions Seuil, undated), p. 21.

4   Rene Bazin, *Charles de Foucauld, Hermit and African Explorer,* Peter Keelan (trans.) (London: Burns & Oates, 1923; second edition, 1931), p. 107.
5   Ibid., p. 110.
6   Ibid., p. 111.
7   *Meditations,* op. cit., p. 41f.
8   *Meditations,* op. cit., p. 45.
9   *Meditations,* op. cit., p. 48f.
10   *Meditations,* op. cit., p. 183.
11   *Meditations,* op. cit., p. 186.

Chapter 8

The Christ of Psalms

Within scripture there is an area of imaginative writing that has encouraged the experience of God to be felt not just in law and promise or miracle and victory, but also through insight and image. Such works come through the grassroots of human feeling and are offered to God for his blessing. They cover a wide range of texts and some of the most beautiful parts of the Bible come within this range. The Psalms are about every conceivable way of relating between God and his people, from the depths of despair to the heights of ecstasy. The 'Song of Songs' describes the love affair with God through the lens of a human romance. The 'Wisdom of Solomon' evokes wisdom in feminine form:

> For she is a breath of the power of God,
> and a pure emanation of the glory of the Almighty.
> (Wis. 7.25)

and she comes forth from God to dwell among men that she may make those who receive her 'friends of God'.

Literature not only formed the minds and hearts of Jewish readers, but continues to influence all who have read and are informed by scripture. The Psalms are the most obvious example of this influence. The words of the Psalms have carved their thoughts on the minds of people ever since they were composed. Many of the Psalms too, throughout history, have been the basis of a personal and community dialogue with God. They breathe life into the prayers of people to this day and will continue to do so as long as faith and doubt, despair and love, and a relationship with God, remain part of the human experience.

The Psalms

The Psalms are poetic and poetry releases the meaning of things to and from the heart. We hear cries of lament and shouts of joy, private musings and public declarations, angry shouts and 'the still small voice of calm'. God is at the centre of these poems, understood in many different ways, and the New Testament feeds from them.

One thing we know from the historical approach to scripture is that within the Bible there are a lot of cross-references from the Old to the New Testament. Matthew's gospel quotes twenty-seven references from the Psalms, eleven of which come from Jesus himself. To understand the way the Psalms move from the Old to the New Testaments we have to turn from a culture in which the use of other people's material is bound by copyright, to a culture where the work of previous generations becomes, quite naturally, the property of another, with little historical distinction or acknowledgement. They are owned by the community; they are a common possession.

The Psalms are a body of poetry containing the religious ideas of many centuries, rather like a hymn book. The disparate groups of Psalms coalesce into one interacting unit of material, 150 of them, drawn on by people in times of joy and of tragedy, when faith is strong, when faith is weak and when people need to worship God publicly or privately. God is a God of all life and of death and of resurrection, and the prayer book of the Jews, the Psalms, enshrines that tradition.

We believe it to have been a resource that Jesus used frequently, partly because it is recorded that he quotes the Psalms in the gospels and also because the evangelists resort to the Psalms so frequently as they bind together various strands of meaning in their work. The most significant evidence, however, is that we know the Psalms were the staple diet of synagogue worship and Jesus, brought up to attend worship, would have absorbed these and many other prayers from the long tradition of Psalm and proverb.

The Psalms in Matthew's gospel

Matthew in his gospel, although he is noted as being the evangelist most critical of the Jewish tradition, has a strong Jewish resonance. In particular, verses from the Psalms have provided Matthew with detail that he has incorporated into his life of Jesus. For example, at Jesus' birth:

> The kings of Tarshish and the Isles shall pay tribute;
> the kings of Sheba and Seba shall bring gifts.
> All kings shall fall down before him;
> all nations shall do him service.
> For he shall deliver the poor that cry out,
> the needy and those who have no helper.
> He shall have pity on the weak and poor;
> he shall preserve the lives of the needy.
> (Ps. 72.10–15)

The visit of the kings to Jesus at his birth reflects the actions of the kings in this Psalm. The combination of a royal welcome and the nature of the one who is worshipped, delivering the poor and having pity on the weak, mirrors exactly what was to be the nature of Jesus, who lies at the centre of Matthew's gospel. We shall see this process time and again in each of the gospels. It is strange for us who work with such an historical mind. We wonder how a Psalm, written possibly 800 years before the birth of Christ, could be so accurate. Then we consider whether Matthew used the Psalm to add lustre to his story of the birth of Jesus, to give it credence with the Jews, rather than describing the visit of the shepherds, as Luke does. The Church, in its wisdom, allows for two visits to Jesus at his birth, the shepherds on the night of the birth, and the kings a few days later on the feast of Epiphany. The early writers of the stories were working with different criteria from those we expect today. The Psalms were not drawn on to make fiction fact. All scripture was resonant with the purposes of God and literalism was not really part of their experience. Any resonance they could find that added to an aspect of Christ's nature as Messiah or Saviour, King or Prophet, from whatever era of history, was a resource for the evangelists.

To enter into the minds of the evangelists we have to set aside some of our modern literalism and allow different considerations to set the agenda. We also have to understand that the holy books of the Bible speak to one another across the generations: Isaiah foresaw the coming of the Messiah, Jesus was the Son of David, Adam was reborn in the death of Jesus as Adam's fault was wiped away. Using the Psalms, we can no longer enter into the spirit of them and expect them to work on a purely linear or horizontal level. We have to enter into them with the eyes of faith and with an understanding of history that puts saving acts over against acts of unbelief. That explains the paradox of Jesus' words, 'Before Abraham was, I am' (Jn. 8.58). If we can understand that, then we can begin to understand the way in which the Psalms are used, in this case to give homage to Jesus and fill out the nature of his divinity.

At the baptism of Jesus, God is given to speak with the words of Psalm 2.7: 'This is my beloved with whom I am well pleased'. There are various ways in which Matthew crafted the Psalms into his gospel. The variety results from the flow of quotations that pervaded the whole of religious life at the time. We have to imagine a multilayered use of the Psalms. Most interesting for understanding the mind of Christ is to locate which of the Psalms Jesus took to himself. Which ones did he mould into his own identity so that he was formed by them and could accurately express his own inner feelings, could carry right through his short life when he used them? This process became particularly important at the time of his passion, and in the circumstances surrounding it.

In the Sermon on the Mount Jesus reflects on those who are loved by God and who reflect the love of God in action. Are they not the poor? Yes indeed, for blessed are the poor. The Psalms provide Jesus directly with two of the beatitudes, those who are pure in heart (Ps. 51.12), and those who mourn (Ps. 126.5). Public worship and private prayer based on the Psalms formed Jesus' soul and filled his mind. So when it came to the experience of suffering at the time of the passion, beginning with the entry into Jerusalem, the Psalms became a main feature of the people's chants and of Jesus' laments. The crowd shouted out words from Psalm 118, 'Blessed is he who comes in the name of the Lord, Hosanna in the Highest'. At the Last Supper there was a reference to the use of the special 'Praise', or in Hebrew *Hallel*, Psalms (Pss. 113–18): 'when they had sung the Psalm, they went out to the Mount of Olives' (Mt. 26.29–30). These Psalms were recited at most of the principal Jewish festivals and during the Passover meal and are thought to have been the hymns sung by Christ and the Apostles after the Last Supper. Psalm 136 is called the 'Great *Hallel*'.

It is the interweaving of the Psalms through the passion narrative that provides one of the most enthralling clues to the way the evangelists understood what Jesus was doing and how they decided to interpret that. The passion story began in Gethsemane for Matthew when Jesus used the words of Psalm 43, which were no doubt churning around in his distressed soul: 'why are you so full of heaviness, O my soul? And why are you so disquieted within me?' (Ps. 43.5). The only other phrase from the Psalms used by Jesus in Matthew's gospel was the cry from the cross 'My God, my God why have you forsaken me?' (Ps. 69.21), another questioning cry from a broken heart.

There is a huge mystery here as we listen to these words from Jesus, who in life seemed to have such a strong faith in God. The crucifixion was altogether a different experience, out of all proportion in terms of human suffering to what had gone before. These words came from the long tradition of lament and they came out as prayers do when they are so well known and embedded in the heart.

The records of these few days and long hours were gathered from several sources and not all the sources agree exactly in the details of the crucifixion. This is not surprising. One person hears and remembers one thing, someone else another. In addition, when the records were written some time after the crucifixion and in the light of Jesus' resurrection appearances, different perceptions of the significance of what took place were put into circulation. Luke's gospel for example has no record of Jesus using the Psalm lament 'My God, My God, why have you forsaken me?', nor does he record the words from Psalm 31.5, 'Into your hands I commend my spirit.' Instead, Luke drew on the Psalms that suited his particular view of Jesus.

The Psalms in Luke's gospel

Luke drew heavily on the Psalms for the songs at the beginning of his gospel, known as the 'Magnificat,' or the 'Song of Mary', and for the 'Benedictus,' or the 'Prophecy of Zechariah'. He placed a Psalm phrase into the mind of the tax collector who would not even look up to heaven, but who beat his breast saying 'God be merciful to me a sinner' (Lk. 18.31; Ps. 51.1.) The prodigal son decided to return home and chose the words he would say to his father when he got there: 'Father, I have sinned against heaven and against you' (Lk. 15.18; Ps. 51.4). When Jesus cast his eyes over Jerusalem, inevitably the Psalms that were chanted within its walls came to his mind. He remembered: 'people will faint from fear and foreboding of what is coming on the world for the powers of heaven will be shaken' which echoes the Psalm 'those who dwell at the ends of the earth tremble at your marvels' (Lk. 21.26; Ps. 65.7).

When it came to writing the passion narratives Matthew, Mark and Luke showed a remarkable similarity in their use of Psalms. It is believed that Mark's gospel provided a source for Matthew and Luke, but it is hard to imagine why Luke omitted the cry of dereliction that seems such a precious remembrance of the suffering of Christ. Perhaps he felt it was too sad for his readers and wished them to remember Jesus who committing his suffering to his heavenly Father, and so Luke recorded these final words: 'Father, into your hands I commend my spirit.' (Lk. 24.46). However, a note of dereliction does come into Luke which did not come into the other accounts. Luke recalled that those who followed Jesus from Jerusalem and who 'stood by at some distance, watching' (Lk. 23.35) echoing the same feeling in Psalm 38.11 'My neighbours stand afar off: my friends and my companions stand apart from my affliction'.

The Psalms in John's gospel

Whereas Matthew, Mark and Luke show a reasonable amount of unanimity when drawing on the Psalms, John is more idiosyncratic, both in the main part of his gospel and in the passion narrative. Some would say this is because John was an eyewitness of the events and therefore had first-hand information. Others would argue that his gospel is the most theological of all and therefore was inspired, not by a concern for exact reporting, but by spiritual themes which penetrate to an inner truth of the nature of Jesus in relation to the Father.

John slipped a Psalm quotation into his philosophical prologue. The 'mercy and truth' of the Psalm have indeed 'met together' in Christ; or as John put it, Jesus is 'full of grace and truth'. (Jn. 1.17; Ps. 25.10). Andrew says to his brother Simon Peter that he has found the Messiah. John explains the meaning of the title Messiah – the Anointed – to remind us of the future destiny of Jesus hinted at in Psalm 2: 'The kings of the earth will rise up and the rulers take counsel together, against the Lord and against his *anointed*' (Jn. 1.41; Ps. 2.2). When Jesus turns over the tables of the moneylenders in the Temple, the disciples recall the words 'Zeal for your house has consumed me' (Jn. 2.17; Ps. 69.10).

John's great literary skill, and the depth of his commitment to the Lord, allowed him to make use of some fundamental images in his gospel. These may well have been sparked by Jesus' own use of familiar everyday words to help people look deeper into God. So we find his sources and see his mind at work with words like bread (Ps. 78.24); gate (Ps. 118.20); shepherd (Ps. 23.1); vine (Ps. 80.9); and priest (Ps. 110.4).

In the description leading up to the crucifixion, John heightened the sense of hatred that Jesus had to suffer from the actions and voices of 'the world'. Indeed 'they hated him without a cause' (Jn. 15.25; Pss. 35.20, 69.4). In the memories of Matthew and Luke, Jesus' garments were divided by the soldiers, but John has the soldiers keeping the garment whole and dicing for the privilege of owning it. John often has extra details that convey inside information and from his gospel we are led to believe he was himself at the foot of the cross. The matter of the garments seems to have emerged from Psalm 22.18: 'They divide my garments among them'. John remembers Jesus being thirsty as the psalmist says 'my mouth is dried up like a pot-sherd' (22.15a) and Jesus' legs were left unbroken as the psalmist foretold, 'He keeps all their bones; so that not one of them is broken' (Ps. 34.20).

From very early on the Psalms have been attributed to David, the saintly scholar king, the boy who slew Goliath, loved Jonathan and dreamt of a Temple to house the holiness of God. David became a role model for Jesus and the Psalms would have helped him enter more closely into that imaginative relationship. Jesus' study of the Psalms would not necessarily have been that much different from ours, except of course for the Hebrew language in which they were written. At their heart the Psalms are about understanding and entering into a relationship with God, a way of getting to know more about how God thinks, acts, feels and responds. Jesus entered into that relationship with great devotion and acumen, as we can too. He would have been saddened by those things that caused God to reject people and which may have been the stimulus to be a bridge between the mercy of God and his people.

It seems strange to talk of changing the mind of God. Yet isn't that exactly what was happening in this amazing period of time when Jesus of Nazareth was turning the understanding of people towards a deeper knowledge of the love of God and initiating the mind and purposes of God in a move towards forgiveness? As Jesus absorbed the Psalms, he was also in practice preparing to assist God in removing the obstacle of sin which prevented people from experiencing his love. Jesus assisted God as a child can assist a parent, showing us a world which contains all that prevents the love of God from transforming the world and showing us the love and sacrifice which overcome those things that prevent us from seeing God's real purpose.

The Psalms are among the documents that show most closely the springboard that moved Jesus into attending on God and assisted his understanding of God's purposes and nature. Jesus' proximity to God allowed him to live the Psalms through his life and in his death. Unique in history, unique in the history of love, unique in our understanding of the purposes of God, the Psalms are the gateway for entry into the mystery of the work of Jesus. We can imagine him absorbing them, taking them in his mind out of the synagogue and chewing them over. We can see him setting them against the world as it was, so much the same then in terms of love, hate, joy, suspicion and ignorance as it is today.

***

The Psalms have been very significant in enriching the prayer life of the church, not least within the monastic orders. The Benedictine tradition understood the reciting of the Psalms as their 'work' and regularly through the day and night this work was done to the glory of God: 'seven times a day shall I praise you' (Ps. 119.164). Benedict of Nursia (c.480–c.550) in his Rule, writes: 'We shall observe this sacred number of seven, if we fulfil the duties of our service in the Hours of Lauds, Prime, Terce, Sext, None, Vespers, and Compline; for it was of these day hours that he said: *Seven times a day have I given praise to you.* But of the night office the same prophet David said: *At midnight will I rise to give you thanks.* At these times, therefore, let us give praise to our Creator *for his righteous judgements* (Ps. 119.62): . . . and let us rise in the night to praise him'. The Psalms, then, were the life-blood of monastic spirituality.

The Psalms are a combination of the opening of the mind of God to the world and the opening of the world's cries to God.

They are a two-way conversation, into which we listen, so that the psalmist's conversation becomes ours, his anger our anger, his praise our praise. The Trappist monk, Thomas Merton (1914–1968) a Cistercian monk, found much solace and inspiration in the Psalms. His diaries and his more formal writings are full of references to them.

In a short booklet, *The Psalms are our Prayer,* Merton wrote:

In the Psalms, we drink divine praise at its pure and stainless source in all primitive sincerity and perfection. We return to the youthful strength and directness with which the ancient psalmists voiced their adoration of the God of Israel. Their adoration was intensified by the ineffable accents of a new discovery: for the Psalms are the songs of men who knew who God was.

If we are to pray well, we too must discover the Lord to whom we speak, and if we use the Psalms in our prayer we will stand a better chance of sharing in the discovery which lies hidden in their words for all generations. For God has willed to make Himself known to us in the mystery of the Psalms.[1]

Reading and meditating on the Psalms from within the Body of Christ, Merton was conscious that these gathered religious outpourings were not speaking directly from their authors, but were being heard and spoken through the events of the incarnation, death and resurrection of Jesus Christ. This is how he presents the seachange:

But God has given Himself to us in Christ. The Psalms are full of the Incarnate Word. Not only is David a 'type' of Christ, but the whole Psalter has always been regarded by the Church, in her liturgy, as though it were a summary and compendium of all that God has revealed. In other words the Psalms contain in themselves all the Old and New Testaments, the whole Mystery of Christ. In singing the

Psalms each day, the Church is therefore singing the
wedding hymn of her union of God in Christ.

To put it very plainly: the Church loves the Psalms
because in them she sings of her experience of God, of her
union with the Incarnate Word, of her contemplation of God
in the Mystery of Christ.[2]

Merton was conscious of having used the Psalms, and having been
used by them, and of the variety of states of being to which they
speak. At the end of the pamphlet Merton directs us to Psalms
that reflect particular aspects of the spiritual journey, such as 'help
needed in affliction' (Ps. 28.1–3):

> To you I call, O Lord my rock
> be not deaf to my cry;
> Lest if you do not hear me
> I become like those who go down to the pit.

To continue in a translation of the Psalms by Mgr Ronald Knox
whose version is used in the pamphlet and which Merton knew
well:

Listen, Lord to my plea as I call upon thee,
as I raise my hand in prayer towards thy holy temple.
Do not summon me, with the wicked, before thy judgement-seat;
with men who traffic in iniquity.[3]

Merton concludes the pamphlet with these words, 'In the last
analysis, it is not so much what we get out of the Psalms that
rewards us, as what we put into them. If we really make them
our prayer, really prefer them to other methods and expedi-
ents, in order to let God pray in us in His own words, and if
we sincerely desire above all to offer Him this particular pure
homage of our Christian faith, then indeed we will enter into the
meaning of the Psalms and they will become our favourite vocal
prayers.'[4]

Notes

1   Thomas Merton, *The Psalms are our Prayer* (London: Burns & Oates, 1957; reprinted in 1977 by Sheldon Press with the title *On the Psalms*), pp. 5, 6.

2   Ibid., p. 7.

3   Ibid., p. 33.

4   Ibid., p. 42.

Chapter 9

The wisdom of Christ

Thomas Merton's immersion into the world of the Psalms came as a result of his daily routine of prayer within the Cistercian monastic tradition, but there was far more than the Psalms to bring him close to the mind of Christ. There was the whole world of 'wisdom' which particularly from the Old Testament and then in later years from various spiritual traditions, helped many to broaden their understanding of the Spirit of Christ. What was the journey that Merton took that made him the best-known contemplative monk of the twentieth century?

Merton was born in France in 1915. His mother was a Quaker, and his father an agnostic; and both were painters. Merton's mother died when he was four and his father died when Tom was fifteen. At the time of his father's death, Tom was at school in Oakham, England. His sense of isolation in the world was ameliorated by a lively enquiring mind and covered up by some wild escapades at university in Cambridge in the 1930s. Leaving Cambridge early on the advice of his guardian and as a result of fathering a child, he left for America where his mother's relations still lived.

Merton continued his studies at Columbia University. He read and wrote a lot and continued a reckless, fun-loving existence. His early life, in terms of high living, was reminiscent of the lives of St Augustine and St Francis. However, searching for something deeper and stronger in which to root his life, Merton responded to an inner call to enter Corpus Christi church in New York and there he found a spiritual home. This conversion opened up for him a whole world of Catholic spirituality. Encouraged by his friends with whom he still maintained a very creative set of relationships, he pursued his new-found faith and felt a calling to the Franciscan Order.

For one reason or another this request was blocked so instead, in 1941, he worked for a while at Friendship House in Harlem, an urban centre run by a lay Catholic community inspired by Dorothy Day and Catherine de Hueck Doherty. Eventually the monastic call was heard again, this time to the Cistercian Order, and in 1941 he entered the monastery of Gethsemane in Kentucky, where, despite many fantasies of moving, he remained until 1968. It was on a trip to Bangkok in December 1968 that he met his tragic, accidental death.

It was while I was still at school and having just two periods of time allotted to going out to the village between four and five o'clock, I decided to go into the public library. I had never heard of Merton, but using the spaces between the shelves to spy on the young female librarians, my eye slipped sideways to the cover of a book, set up on the shelf to show its front. The cover showed a monk staring out over a forest. There was something hugely attractive to me about this picture. The mood was quiet, peaceful and thoughtful, and all those abstract feelings were focused onto a person intent on contemplation. I borrowed the book from the library. It was summer and warm, so I went into the churchyard of the parish church and read bits of it. It was utterly compelling. 'There is no true spiritual life outside the love of Christ. We have a spiritual life only because we are loved by him.'[1] 'The solitary life is above all a life of prayer'.[2] 'When I am liberated by silence, when I am no longer involved in the measurement of life, but in the living of it, I can discover a form of prayer in which there is effectively no distraction. My whole life is full of prayer.'[3] There were words like 'silence' I had not heard anyone use creatively before. I had heard them shouted as orders, but never whispered as an invitation. This was in 1963 when I was sixteen. It should have been girls, but actually it was contemplation.

The similarity to St Augustine of Merton's early life came not only in his waywardness but also in his genius for self-reflection and voracious appetite for writing and reading. *The Confessions* of

Augustine and Merton's *The Seven Storey Mountain* are compara-
ble in some ways. Both tell remarkable stories of the love affair
with God. Both resourced themselves by a close attention to the
Psalms, and the wisdom literature in general. The Psalter is par
excellence the monastic prayer book and Merton (Father Louis in
the monastery) would have been imbued with its rhythms and its
images of God's nature and activities. He cried from the heart in
the words of the Psalms and expressed his anger with the anger
of the psalmist. The monk could live his life through these verses
and know that generations had been doing the same thing before
them. The community at the Abbey of Gethsemane would have
sung and recited the Psalms in Latin from the Vulgate translation
and that would have given Merton an even closer connection with
the Latin teachers of the Church and the long stretch of medieval
monasticism.

I wanted to discover how 'the mind of Christ' attracted and influenced a twentieth-century monk and to see how Christ found his
place in the agenda of a literary contemplative, open to many of the
influences of a secular age. It seems feeble to say that Christianity
was unfashionable in the 1960s, as if it mattered whether a thing
was fashionable or not, but holding to unfashionable doctrines
and yet still being widely read and appreciated makes Merton a
very interesting case-study. I wanted to see if what mattered to me
mattered also to another and in what way.

Merton's monastic life stretched from 1941 to 1968, which covered three decades of tempestuous social and cultural history in
the West. It included four years of the Second World War and the
dropping of the atom bomb on Hiroshima; the Second Vatican
Council presided over by Pope John XXIII; the war in Vietnam;
the assassinations of Martin Luther King and J. F. Kennedy. On a
personal level Merton spent the 1940s settling into monastic life
and it was in many ways a period of romantic attachment to being
'a monk'. In the 1950s the romance was wearing off and restlessness
was beginning to take over. Should he leave and start a new community in South America? Should he seek greater solitude in his
own community? In fact these dreams became partially realized

as he inhabited from time to time first a railway carriage, then a watchtower in the forest, and then a woodshed he named St Anne. He also began to teach the novices and share with them many of the passions in the world of theology and spirituality that he was himself involved with and was writing about. The 1990s found Merton turning his face to the world and engaging with the volcanic eruption of beat and pop culture, the anti-war lobby and the deepening interest in other world religions. It was at a conference of monastics, where he read a paper on 'Marxism and Monastic Perspectives', that he died.

His understanding of Christ flowed all the way through these packed and highly creative years. Put like that, it sounds as though there was no time for contemplation, but on the contrary, contemplation entered every aspect of his life and set the Word within all the words. In a life that encompassed so much thought, Christ was a constant reality: a reality to whom everything could be referred, in which everything could find a home. Christ would last, even when all the books that Merton read and wrote and skimmed were back in the library. Christ was the human face of God drawing all that he did into the embrace of love. Christ was the Name deeper than the spoken name. After Merton had finished what was to be his final lecture in Bangkok, weary in the sultry heat, he was questioned as to why the audience were asked to speak no more of Christ, when they had been sent for that very purpose? A tired Fr Louis answered, 'What we are asked to do at present is not so much to speak of Christ as to let Him live in us, so that people may find Him by feeling how He lives in us'.[4]

For Merton, as for the poet Gerard Manley Hopkins, 'Christ plays in ten thousand places'. We have seen how Christ lives in the Psalms of the Hebrew scriptures, but Merton found the whole of scripture material for contemplation. He wrote, 'Necessity of the Bible. More and more of it...extraordinary riches and delicacy of the varied OT concepts of sin...importance of reading and thinking and keeping silent. Self-effacement not in order to be left looking at oneself but to be found in Christ and lost to the rest. Yet not by refusing to take interest in anything vital.'[5] The scriptures gave a rich insight into the mind of Christ for Merton.

Yet this was not at the expense of his consistent delight in finding
Christ beyond the confines of the scriptures in the natural world,
in contemporary literature, in human contact and among thinkers
all over the world with whom he corresponded.

'Refusing to take interest in anything vital' was not an option for
Merton. He turned to the world from the paradoxical hiddenness
of his monastery and understood the world better than many living more obviously within it. In a fascinating period of his life in the
early part of 1958, on one particular day, he experienced extreme
frustration. He was asked to celebrate at more services than he felt
he could manage, the condition of the forest which he loved was in
an awful mess, and when he went to speak with the Abbot, Dom
James spent most of the time on the telephone. Worst of all, Merton
had just heard that permission for him to help set up a new founda-
tion in South America had been denied. But after all these things,
he had a dream. In his dream the figure of Proverb appeared to him.
Proverb came in the form of a young Jewish girl, who embraced
Merton with an innocent but determined passion. He reflected that
she belonged to the same race as St Anne, which was the name he
had given to his hermitage at the time. Proverb encapsulated all
the wisdom of the Old Testament and, among other things, held
together for Merton the wisdom of all the ages and of every tradition, and she came with such graciousness, in a feminine form.

This dream meeting with Proverb seemed to release in Merton a
whole new source of spiritual energy harnessed in a love towards
the humanity of the world. It was just two weeks later on a visit to
Louisville that he received a vision of oneness with all humanity.
He suddenly realized that he loved all the people and that none
of them were, or could be, totally alien to him. He described this
vision and placed within it the strongest link possible with Christ,
the Word made flesh, of St John's gospel. 'My vocation does not
really make me different from the rest of men or put me in a special
category . . . I am still a member of the human race – and what more
glorious destiny is there for man, since the Word was made flesh
and became, too, a member of the Human Race!' Christ is at the
heart of Merton's incarnational vision, and so is the feminine figure
of Proverb. 'The touch of your hand makes me a different person.

To be with you is rest and truth. Only with you are these things found, dear child sent to me by God.'[6]

Merton was very familiar with the poetry of Hopkins whose vision was similar. Yet he was not in 1958 aware of the writings of the seventeenth-century priest Thomas Traherne although he did later read him and thought him one of the very best and most delightful of Anglican writers. Walking into Hereford, Traherne saw similar things to Merton: 'The city seems to stand in Eden, or to be built in heaven. The streets were mine, as much as theirs, the temple was mine, the people were mine, their clothes and gold and silver were mine, as much as their sparkling eyes, fair skins and ruddy faces. The skies were mine, and so were the sun and moon and stars, and all the world was mine and I the only spectator and enjoyer of it.'[7] Both Traherne and Merton saw the world anew.

For Merton it was the figure of Proverb who united the scriptures, Old and New. Proverb and Christ came to Merton to release him into feeling at one with the whole human race, both Jew and Christian, and later he was to feel a similar bond with the mystics of all the great religions. On the same day as the vision in Louisville he bought a secondhand book called *The Family of Man* for 50 cents. It was a book of photographs created for the Museum of Modern Art, New York, in 1955, with a prologue by Carl Sandburg. In it were some of the most famous photographs of all time. They were of people, of humanity in all its aspects, babies being born, soldiers dying, Einstein in his study, a poor Russian family at table. Merton wrote later in his diary, 'All those fabulous pictures . . . How scandalized some men would be if I said that the whole book is to me a picture of Christ and yet that is the Truth. There, there is Christ in my own kind, my own kind – "kind" which means likeness and which means love.'[8]

The 1960s

The 1960s brought significant new developments in Merton's thinking about Christ in the context of his monastic life. Pop culture, the growing interest in faith traditions other than Christianity, the war in Vietnam and his own emotional encounter with a real Proverb, in the form of a nurse whom he met in hospital, all contributed to a deep revaluation of the place of Christ in the modern world. Where then was Christ in all of this?

Between October 1967 and his death in December 1968, we would expect to find a difference in Merton's Christology, and it certainly was dramatically different. The few references to Christianity are blunt. 'A retreat conductor started out by saying Buddhists are life-denying and Christians are life-affirming. I couldn't care less about such platitudes. What does he mean by life?'[9] 'The sick distortion of Christianity is deep in all the thinking of the war-makers.'[10] On the night of the assassination of Martin Luther King, he wrote, 'Is the Christian message of love a pitiful delusion? Or must one "just" love in an impossible situation? And what sense can possibly be made by an authoritarian Church that comes out 100 years late with its official pronouncements?'[11]

In the course of 1968 Merton made several journeys to stay with other religious communities around the world: to the Pacific shore, to New Mexico, to Alaska and then between October and December 1968, to the Far East. It was this final journey that attracted so much interest with regard to his state of mind about the relationship of Christianity to Hinduism and Buddhism. The evidence of the diaries suggests that Merton was largely consumed with listening, looking and learning. The digesting of such a wealth of experience was going to take considerable time. Tragically it was not going to be possible to offer the world an organized Christology on his return, for he never did return. He died from electrocution in his room in Bangkok just after delivering his paper to the Conference of Abbots.

If Merton had returned to Gethsemane I wonder where his love of Christ might have been manifested and his prophetic role would have led us? I hazard a guess that it might have led us deeper into a Christ-like love, sharing with all peace-loving people of whatever religion a wider vision of unity 'in Christ'. The figure of Proverb – gentle, loving and feminine – helped Merton to complement a life that had been male-dominated in many ways. Proverb was also a Holy Spirit presence for him and a mother. His own mother, Ruth, who had encouraged him so much in his early years with language and with art and painting, died when Merton was six. Proverb emerged at a time when his life began to be transformed into a commitment to the world. He did this paradoxically by narrowing the focus of his external circumstances and settling into a hermitage in the extensive grounds of the monastery, but his heart, mind and soul were hungry for contact with everyone who spoke to him of the Spirit.

Etty Hillesum: Proverb in Amsterdam

There is no practical link at all between Thomas Merton and Etty Hillesum, except that they were both diarists and they both liked Rilke's poetry. In my own mind they are linked by Proverb. Etty was Jewish, but there is no sense that she practised her faith; there are no diary entries about her attending synagogue. However, the strong sense of feminine wisdom that emerges from the writings of Etty leads me to hold her together with Merton. In the years 1941–3 of Etty's diaries, Merton was just beginning his novitiate at Gethsemane. Etty was spending her last years in Amsterdam before being transported first to Westerbork and then to Auschwitz. She was born on 15 January 1914, in Middelburg; Merton was born on the last day of January 1915 in Prades, France.

Etty (Esther) began her diary-writing when her life took a romantic turn and she fell in love with German chirologist, Julius Spier (1887–1942). Spier (S. in the diaries) counselled people by studying their hands. Etty's father was a teacher, but had retired by the time the diary began. Her mother, Etty said, was a shambles, but loving and hospitable. Her brothers were academically clever and the household was richly musical.

It may well have been Julius Spier who encouraged Etty to begin a diary. Her first entry on Saturday 8 March 1941 begins with a letter addressed to 'Dear Herr S . . . ' expressing her love for him.

Written in a series of exercise books, the diary is a record of a remarkable woman, full of ups and downs, depressions and exaltations, and so human, vulnerable, giving, loving both sexually and with tremendous self-giving love and compassion for others. There is nothing of the plaster saint about her. The diary charts a progress into deeper understanding and commitment to Christ from within her Jewish roots and her main teacher in this was Dr Spier.

I am much reminded of Merton's Proverb when I read Etty's diary. This is not because of her statuesque, dream-like quality – Etty was full of very down-to-earth human contradictions – but because of her capacity for self-knowledge and love. Proverb came to Merton. Etty, often shy, withdrawn and full of doubt gave of herself to others, and in the form of her diaries gave herself to the world.

There are constant references in the diaries to Rilke, whose poems are of deep 'inwardness' yet relate to such strong and simple images, appealed very much to her, as they did to Merton. Obviously the relationship with Dr Spier is the overriding theme of the diaries and that too troubled her at times. She is ambivalent. He was a married man whose wife lived in England and occasionally she thought of giving up the relationship, but she could not and always saw it as one of compassion, and reserved her greater love for God. After Spier's death in 1942, she wrote, 'God and I have been left behind alone, and there is no one else left to help me . . . It doesn't make me feel impoverished at all, rather quite rich and peaceful. God and I have been left behind all alone. Good night.'[12]

Her great revelation early on in the diary was her desire 'to kneel down'.

24 September, 1941: And now I have that solemn feeling again: I must set about everything afresh once more. I don't think I've been working on myself with the necessary seriousness of late. I thought that I could carry on as I am. This afternoon I suddenly found myself kneeling on the brown coconut matting in the bathroom, my head hidden in

my dressing gown, which was slung over the broken cane chair. Kneeling doesn't really come easily to me, I feel a sort of embarrassment. Why? Probably because of the critical, rational, aesthetic bit that is part of me as well... and yet every so often I have a great urge to kneel down with my face in my hands and in this way to find some peace and to listen to that hidden source within me.[13]

The body has a very important part to play in the sacrament of a love for God. Proverb appeared in human form although in a dream. Wisdom came incarnate, and so it was with her body that Etty began her love affair with God. Somehow the bathroom has a strange, almost humorous ring to it, but it was probably one of the quieter and more secret parts of the house. 'I have two great feelings deep inside: love, an inexplicable love, which cannot be analysed because it is so primitive, for creatures and for God or for what I call God; and compassion, a boundless compassion that can sometimes cause tears to spring from my eyes.'[14]

Etty was much concerned about the things her body did, and given her human frame she understood that living religiously was a way of conducting a bodily life. She didn't see her body as a mass of stuff, but as a space into which she could place the needs of others and a shape that she could offer to God. Her kneeling was her offering. She could have chosen not to kneel, but she chose to kneel. The kneeling was a gift to God, a sacrificial offering, and as she offered she also received the capacity to hear the hidden source within. This space within was not only a meditative space. It was a place where compassion could grow. As the time came for the inevitable journey towards death in the concentration camp, that space had more work to take on. It had to take on the sufferings of others. It had to 'clear a space for sorrow.'

28 March 1942: Ought we not from time to time open ourselves up to cosmic sadness? One day I shall surely be able to say, Yes your life is beautiful, and I value it anew at the end of every day, even being murdered in concentration

camps. And you must be able to bear your sorrow; even if it seems to crush you, you will be able to stand up again, for human beings are so strong: and your sorrow must become an integral part of yourself; part of your body and your soul, you mustn't run away from it, but bear it like an adult. Do not relieve your feelings through hatred, do not seek to be avenged on all German mothers, for they too, sorrow at this very moment for their slain and murdered sons. Give your sorrow all the space and shelter in yourself that is its due, for if everyone bears his grief honestly and courageously, the sorrow that now fills the world will abate. But if you do not clear a decent shelter for your sorrow, and instead reserve most of the space inside you for thoughts of hatred and revenge – from which new sorrows will be born for others – then sorrow will never cease in this world and will multiply. And if you have given sorrow the space its gentle origins demand, then you may truly say: life is beautiful and so rich. So beautiful and so rich that it makes you want to believe in God.[15]

It was inevitable that as a Jew, Etty would be sent off to an extermination camp. It had been expected for many months. Friends of hers had already gone. Etty wrote, 'Be confident and prepared. I shall now see to my rucksack. Oh if only one could let one's heart fly like a bird through everything that happens! What I fear most is numbness, and all those people with whom I shall be herded together: – And yet there must be someone to live through it all and bear witness to the fact that God lived, even in these times. And why should I not be that witness.'[16]

Rowan Williams has this to say about Etty:

The pattern of a physical life traces the outline, so to speak, of a discovered object, which is made visible only by the continuous policy of 'tracing'. Beginning with the conscious practice of such a pattern, a whole biography can take on the same character, to become a symbolic outline. Etty Hillesum learns to kneel, and learns in due course to plot her location within the tumultuous spiritual geography of the Gestapo office and the camp at Westerbork... We begin to learn how to be a sign inhabited by God's meanings as we accept a shape for our physical practice that arises in response to the sort of pressure Etty Hillesum charts, the pressure of a passion for transparency to oneself and truthful feeling.[17]

Etty's diaries are so compelling because they are working from a position of vulnerability, of not knowing, of humility, and as we read we are able to learn and experience with her. Not only did she let in those around her, but her tracing, her pattern, is exposed to us many years later through her writing.

Her body got tired, but it was at that point that she felt the Spirit was taking over. Whatever else was happening, the Spirit could do its work. It could love. This comes very close to the idea of that great Jewish mind, Paul, where the spirit communicates with the Spirit of God. Etty writes: 'if I say that I *hearken*, it is really God who hearkens inside me. The most essential and the deepest in me hearkening unto the most essential and deepest in the other. God to God.'[18]

In the camp at Westerbork she was completely at her wits' end, but 'then I have my folded hands and bended knee. A posture that is not handed down from generation to generation with us Jews. I have had to learn it the hard way. It is my most precious inheritance from the man whose name I have almost forgotten... What a strange story it really is, my story. The girl who could not kneel. Or its variation: the girl who learned to pray. That is my most intimate gesture.'[19]

Etty's final communication with the outside world was a scribbled note posted through the slats in her carriage about to leave for Auschwitz. It was to her friend Christine van Nooten. '*Near Glimmen, Tuesday, 7 September 1943*. Christine, opening the Bible at random I find this: "The Lord is my high tower". I am sitting on my rucksack in the middle of a full freight car. Father, Mother, and Mischa are a few cars away. In the end, the departure came without warning. On sudden special orders from The Hague. We left the camp singing... Etty.'[20]

Notes

1 Thomas Merton, *Thoughts in Solitude* (London: Burns & Oates, 1958), p. 32.
2 Ibid., p. 86.
3 Ibid., p. 78.
4 *The Thomas Merton Studies Center*, 'Concerning the Collection in the Bellarmine College Library – A Statement, November 10, 1963', by Thomas Merton, John Howard Griffin and Msgr. Alfred F. Horrigan, (Santa Barbara: Unicorn Press, 1971).
5 *A Search for Solitude, The Journals of Thomas Merton, Volume Three, 1952–1960*, Lawrence S. Cunningham (ed.) (New York: HarperCollins, 1996), p. 135.
6 Ibid., p.182.
7 Thomas Traherne, *Centuries of Meditations* (published and edited by Bertram Dobell, London, 1908), p. 158.
8 *A Search for Solitude*, op. cit., p. 182.
9 *The Other Side of the Mountain, The Journals of Thomas Merton, Volume Seven, 1967–1968*, Patrick Hart, O.C.S.O. (ed.) (London: HarperCollins, 1998), p. 44.
10 Ibid., p. 62.
11 Ibid., p. 78.
12 *ETTY, The Letters and Diaries of Etty Hillesum 1941–1943*, Klaas A.D. Smelik (ed.), Arnold J. Pomerans (trans.) (Grand Rapids, MI: Eerdmans, 2002), p. 544.
13 Ibid., p. 103.
14 Ibid., p. 161.
15 Ibid., pp. 308, 309.
16 Ibid., p. 506.
17 Rowan Williams, 'Religious Lives', Romanes Lecture, 18 November 2004, Oxford, taken from transcript.
18 *ETTY*, op. cit., p. 519.
19 Ibid., p. 547.
20 Ibid., pp. 658, 659.

Chapter 10

Christ minds: The St John Passion

In the beginning

I want to take you back to the beginning and first your beginning. First memories. Walking along a sunlit suburban road, walking on the low wall to school. A road and the corner of the road and a school. The school has the alphabet on the wall and there is a piano. I don't go back much before that, except not being able to sleep and getting into my parents' bed and my father having to shift out elsewhere. Not very surprising, or telling, but they are beginnings, first apprehensions of something rather than nothing, of life, of existence, of being a person, though I didn't think then 'Aha! I am having my first thoughts'. Thinking about thinking comes later. But it is remarkable what we can do and thinking and remembering are two of the remarkable things. Then there's knowing that we are feeling something and being able to say things and name things. The two-year-old Thomas Merton used to rush around his garden in France shouting 'Oh sun! Oh joli!' But if we just think back to our earliest memories, we enter a world of great wonder and mystery; of being human, of having thoughts and sharing them in words, of talking with others.

In the beginning was thought. In the beginning was the ability to wonder, to dream, to speak, to be aware, to be aware of being at all. That's where we begin and that's where St John wanted to begin his gospel, for if there is no wonder at being at all, then there is no wonder at there being God. John laid at the feet of God the wonder of being. God's great gift was creating being: 'In the beginning was the word' (Jn. 1.1): words of God which said yes, and go, and be, and love, and praise.

The Greek word is 'logos', from which we get our English words logical, logo and logarithm. Logos meant far more than just 'word'. It meant meaning. Meaningless chatter can sound like words but without meaning, a word is not *the* word. We can get fed up with a welter of words. Samuel Beckett is the great modern master of showing how words can just get too much. St John is consciously beginning his work, his gospel, with a reference to the beginning of Genesis: 'In the beginning God created the heavens and the earth' (Gen. 1.1). God's word spoke creation into being. But John was concerned with a new creation, not a later one, and one that had been from the very beginning with God, yet had taken its time to appear. John was talking about a personal being in whom was 'life'. There had been life before, but this was a new kind of life, which was as remarkable a creation as the light that God had made. This light was the light that lit up the nature of what a person truly was, the charge that made people special within creation, with special abilities and special responsibilities, with the power to make, to think, to love, to wonder, to destroy, to cause pain and to muck up. Into that world came Jesus, the Word, who at first could not speak a word.

Something strange and wonderful was emerging, but it was also challenging and mysterious. With John's gospel we get this unusual combination of the utmost clarity of detail alongside enigma, strangeness, things just out of reach. Jesus is as real as you could wish one minute, real as any other person, and yet continually saying things so that we are left wondering, 'what *does* he mean by that?' 'My hour has not yet come' (Jn. 2.4). What was this hour? When was it coming? What did he mean, 'My hour has not yet come'?

But we want to know, because we love the one who says these things and we are hungry and thirsty for every crumb of detail about someone we love: no fact too small, no strand of hair too trivial, when we love them. The details and the mystery are to come in plenty. Take light for example. Light is a picture of one of the aspects of Jesus. He is 'the light of the world'. If we are really grateful for light to bring the day, the warmth and the ability to see in the natural world, then we will understand how important the light is. Similarly, Jesus the light of the world helps us understand God.

The prologue to John's gospel (1.1–14) is like the overture of a symphony. It sets out the basic themes in the work to come. Jesus is 'the true light which enlightens everyone and he was coming into the world.' However, the overture sounds a warning note, a note of sadness. We have to expect tragedy. 'Jesus was in the world and the world came into being through him; yet the world did not know him. He came to what was his own, and his own people did not accept him' (1.10). It has to be said that some of the most self-consciously religious people of the time could not understand how God could choose this particular person, Jesus, to be anything special.

The secret of the acceptance of Jesus as being 'one with God' lies in the idea of 'faith'. There is no other criterion. Inside information is no good. Intellectual status is no good. Religious background is no good. Faith is the secret of acceptance – faith without knowing, without status, without pedigree. A leap into the light is what we are called to make if we want to be children of God. But 'now is the hour' for the leap. I look at that word 'logos' and I see it as so contemporary, so 'now'. We all understand if a machine or a garment has a 'logo'. It is a label with a message, a name, a sign, a word or picture. Jesus is the 'logos' of God.

What the modern world has not taken to its heart, 'except those that receive him' is the full impact of v. 14 in the prologue of John: 'And the Logos (the label, the word) became flesh'. John could not explain Jesus' nature better than to say, this person Jesus puts flesh on the idea of God. He came and lived among us and we saw the glory of God shine in him, the glory you might well expect from the only Son of God, full of grace and truth. The words on the page are numinous, but until they put on flesh and come and live in human form as we live in human form, then they are empty words. 'The Word became flesh' (1.14) resonates partly because we know what happened to the flesh. We know who it was that returned to his mother's arms beneath the cross of Calvary.

Eternal life

We have been with Christ for some time already, some of us for decades, some of us less. We have followed him through some tough times and we have begun to understand a little of what he means when he shares with us insights into his relationship with his Father. His Father is not in this case Joseph. This Father is altogether different. There is a great intimacy between Jesus and the Father. It is like two threads being twined together. This is how John the evangelist describes it: 'The Son can do nothing on his own but only what he sees the Father doing, for whatever the Father does, the Son does likewise' (Jn. 5.19).

Jesus comes out with some straight talking and he says 'Very truly I say to you', we listen: 'Anyone who hears my word and believes Him who sent me has eternal life and does not come under judgement but has passed from death to life' (Jn. 5.24).

Eternal life is one of those phrases that we hear a lot. When Jesus says it, if we do some imagining, just by the way he says it and looks as he says it and by the tone of his voice we catch a glimpse of what eternal life might be like. We see in eternal life a blessed union, a peace and such a natural being together with someone we love and don't have to strive to make conversation with, or be nice to beyond our range, but can be completely natural with. Yet we worry about how this can go on forever and won't it get awfully tiring being in the same state for years and years? So we get an idea of time which will not stretch out in the way it does here. Time will give way to love and we don't measure love in days, but in depth, closeness and peace. Eternal life will be made up of all those things that don't tire us. On the contrary, eternity will engage our interest and time will cease to matter. It will give way to joy. Eternal life will be to know God (Jn. 17.3).

Eternity remains a little way off yet. 'First the Son of Man must be lifted up, that whoever believes in him may have eternal life' (Jn. 12.34). Before eternal life can be made a reality for those who believe, the crucifixion must take place. As Moses was able to do wonders with the serpent, which was lifted up in the wilderness and became a rod to release the children of Israel through the waters of certain death, so Jesus' crucifixion will release all who believe into freedom, having passed through the waters of baptism. The secret of eternal life lies in Christ. We have to come to him 'to have life' (Jn. 5.39). Before 'the lifting up on the cross' there is a great deal of frustration to undergo and a great deal of teaching to expound.

We might have said, if we had looked carefully at the other evangelists, that we ought to experience the Last Supper as the way of entering into the passion story. Maundy Thursday ushers in Good Friday. However, John takes the celebration of the Last Supper as an established fact of Christian practice, as one of the means to eternal life. So Jesus said to the disciples, 'very truly, I tell you, unless you eat of the flesh of the Son of Man and drink his blood, you have no life in you. Those who eat my flesh and drink my blood have eternal life, and I will raise them up on the last day' (6.54).

For John, the ceremony that initiated the events of the passion was the washing of the feet of the disciples. As the bread and wine of the Passover supper allowed the disciples to enter into the Body of Christ, so acts of loving charity brought them into a close relationship with Jesus. Peter remonstrated against this, but Jesus said 'Unless I wash you, you have no share with me' (Jn. 13.8). By implication, to be 'in Christ' we have to serve each other in love. We must wash the tired and weary feet of the disciples, as they return for mutual support and encouragement.

The sacrament of the Eucharist and the sacrament of love are two ways to the mystery of eternal life. Yet who wants eternal life? Have we not been so excited by the quick-fix rewards of this life, that we long for the rewards that are 'now', what *we* want? Looked at like that, eternal life seems boring by comparison. We are prepared to live for 'kicks' now and take our chance that the future will come to us anyway, without our asking, as part of the package of ordinary life – our rights, so to speak. But again, no. We have got to want to want eternal life and to want to spend our lives engaging in the desire for it and learning how that desire slips in between us and God's grace.

Yet is eternal life a real possibility for us, and if not why do we bother? Yes, it is attainable by us, but here is the mystery. Our attaining it is dependent on our loving the One who can give it. We cannot 'get' eternal life on our own. We have to receive it as a gift from God, but we must love the One who holds the secret to it; and we love not just for gaining the secret; we love the One who holds the secret to eternal life regardless. We love him because he first loved us. A few hours before Jesus was betrayed and arrested in the garden, he looked up to heaven and said to his Father, 'Father, the hour has come; glorify your Son so that the Son may glorify you, since you have given him authority over all people, to give eternal life to all whom you have given him.' (Jn. 17.1–2).

Let not your hearts be troubled

It would be easy to wallow in a sense of despair and gloom at the idea of the death of Christ on the cross, to become professional mourners, to enjoy the black, but beware. A sense of deep serious-ness towards crucifixion is inevitable and right, but we have to see all that takes place on Good Friday through the glory of the resur-rection. We know about the resurrection as an historical event. At the crucifixion of Christ the disciples could not be sure of the fu-ture and therefore had every right to be gloomy and afraid. Yet we need to check this against the record. Jesus was careful throughout his earthly ministry to tell the disciples the whole story. He told them about the suffering that was inevitable, but he added that in three days he would rise again. Jesus had faith in his Father.

Of course, that did not alleviate the physical pain and for Mark in his gospel we hear the real agony of the cross, when Jesus cries out 'My God, My God, why have you forsaken me?' (Mk. 15.34). The mental and physical pain was very real. The wood was hard, the nails were sharp, the crown of thorns was pushed down on his head, but the faith of Christ was profound, fixed on the glory that was to come. Unparalleled words of comfort pour from Jesus in the hours before the crucifixion: 'Do not let not your hearts be troubled. Believe in God, believe also in me. (Jn. 14.1). I will come again and will take you to myself so that where I am, there you may be also.' (Jn. 14.3).

This is not just emotional comfort. Jesus shifts the idea of comfort onto an altogether different plane, away from the vagaries of our emotions and onto the more established plane of truth; of what 'is', whether we are happy or sad. The truth is that Jesus is as close to God as a father is to a son; a closeness which is of the very essence of their mutual indwelling as well as something which we can think of as being like our own a, heart to heart. This closeness to the point of undivided intimacy colours the entire account of the crucifixion, and so faith in the reality of God the Father and God the Son being one turns the crucifixion into a triumph of love rather than leaving it as a tragedy from which no good can come. How often have I tried to put that into words of comfort in the normal pastoral round: at the death of loved ones, through tragedies and with seemingly life-closing disappointments.

In John's characteristic way of setting up questions to invite answers, as Plato or Socrates might have done, Jesus says, 'Do you not believe that I am in the Father and the Father is in me?' (Jn. 14.10). Hearing this makes an enormous difference to our approach to the crucifixion. It does not make us happy in an effervescent way but roots a truth in our whole being. It says that in this person – Jesus – lies the secret to eternal life.

The spiritual writer, Baron von Hügel, wrote to his niece shortly before his death. He was awaiting his end and all his life he had immersed himself in things to do with God, so his words have a particular resonance as we reflect on the final days of Christ's earthly life: 'I wait for the breath of God. Perhaps he will call me today – tonight. Don't let us be niggardly towards God ... Plant yourself on foundations that are secure – God – Christ – Suffering – the Cross. They are secure. Caring is the greatest thing – my faith is not enough, it comes and goes – Keep your life a life of prayer, dearie – Keep it like that: it's the only thing, and remember; no joy without suffering – no patience without trial – no humility without humiliation – no life without death.'[1]

'No life without death' – how rarely we consider that. However much we see the power of God at work in the crucifixion, we must always remember that the cross is a sharp reality. This is why Jesus spends so much time preparing the disciples for the future, when they would be living and working in the realm of faith and depending so much on the Holy Spirit.

'The Advocate, the Holy Spirit, whom the Father will send in my name, will teach you everything, and remind you of all I have said to you. Peace I leave with you; my peace I give to you. I do not give to you as the world gives. Do not let your hearts be troubled, and do not let them be afraid.' (Jn. 14.26–27).

Releasing the spirit

Jesus was quite sure that his death would change things for his disciples. Things would be different. The comfort he had given them through his wisdom and healing miracles would not abruptly cease with his death. On the contrary, his death would release a new sort of power, which would bear a family likeness. 'Now I am going to him who sent me ... nevertheless, I tell you the truth: it is to your advantage that I go away, for if I do not go away, the Advocate will not come to you; but if I go, I will send him to you' (Jn. 16.5–7). 'I will not leave you orphaned' (Jn. 14.18).

This 'Advocate' is the Holy Spirit of God, who will continue the work of Jesus after his death. But John, in his gospel, does not allow us to wallow in false sentiment. The Advocate will come to offer some strong truths and challenge us on the matters of sin, righteousness and judgement. What or who is this Advocate? It is the 'Comforter' of old. A 'comforter' these days is something a child takes with them to bed to help them sleep. Is that it? No, this Comforter is altogether more grown up and to our pampered ears tougher and more challenging. The Comforter demands things from us and challenges us.

We don't like to be challenged. We would rather watch a film where Jesus does all the suffering and we can watch and empathize, but we know we would soon tire of that. (Although, judging by how we can absorb hours of television, there seems to be no limit to the amount of material we can watch without it making a blind bit of difference. It doesn't change our behaviour at all, except to make us duller).

The major thing we are learning from John's gospel about the crucifixion is not to gawk at a horrid sight or gaze in a romantic reverie and see the crucifixion as one more film which we can take or leave. That is not it at all. The crucifixion released the Holy Spirit, the Comforter, to be the human Christ with us, freed from the limitations of the human body, but with the same powerful nature. We get to know more about this Spirit by the life of prayer and by the way each day we are aware of letting God the Holy Spirit have access to our very being, our deep moral being. We let the Spirit in by the springs of our decision-making, our choices and our propensity to love. We allow the Spirit to work as we let it bring before us the serious matters of 'sin, righteousness and judgement' (Jn. 16.8). These are words we do not like and words that we must be very wary indeed of wielding in the face of others.

The Holy Spirit is a wonderful mystery and should never be thinned down in our minds as if it acted without the support of God the Father and God the Son. In the three lies one reality. But what, we cry, does it mean for *us* in reality? These are Gethsemane questions. They are questions that lead, awkwardly and powerfully, into faith. If our life was all planned out as if we were on a conveyor belt, being bolted together to a plan like a motor car, then there would be no possibility of us being what we most miraculously are: human beings. Let us get back for a moment to the beginning and reflect on our essential being. Once *that* wonder is experienced, the moral life is engaged and our decisions for or against the glory of 'our being at all' reveal themselves in joy and in pain. The Holy Spirit settles like the brooding one in our inmost being, encouraging us and helping us to be what God intended for us from the very beginning.

The crucifixion of the Son of God released the possibility of this new life in the Spirit. It was a victory for what is true for everyone, the capacity to know God and live in him. The cross was the pain that all mothers know in bringing a child to life in the world, a new life for all who believe and trust in him.

A little while, and you will no longer see me, and again a little while, and you will see me? Very truly, I tell you, you will weep and mourn, but the world will rejoice; you will have pain, but your pain will turn into joy. When a woman is in labour, she has pain because her hour has come. But when her child is born, she no longer remembers the anguish because of the joy of having brought a human being into the world. So you have pain now; but I will see you again, and your hearts will rejoice, and no one will take your joy from you. On that day you will ask nothing of me. Very truly, I tell you, if you ask anything of the Father in my name, he will give it to you. Until now you have not asked for anything in my name. Ask and you will receive, so that your joy may be complete (Jn. 16.19–24).

'And with ah! bright wings'

We cannot just go on imagining that what happened to Jesus was the same as will happen to us. We have to enter a new world of meaning, another dimension altogether from the one we know. That is going to make ordinary living very difficult, because we have felt the hand of God upon us and we have a huge nostalgia for that hand to touch us again.

It is like love. We enter a dream world in which the hints of eternity in this world become stronger and stronger. How Christ must have longed to be all the time with God the Father; the record of the saints is the same. Once we have known the love of God, glimpsed it if we have the artist's eyes, 'felt' it if we work with our emotions, touched it if we are physical people, then the world becomes a changed place. The poet Hopkins, as we saw before, was not blind to the sordidness and evil of the world and which prevented people from sensing the presence of God because of debilitating conditions; but he had the capacity to see the glory also:

> And for all this, nature is never spent;
>   There lives the dearest freshness deep down things;
> And though the last lights off the black West went
>   Oh, morning, at the brown brink eastward, springs –
> Because the Holy Ghost over the bent
> World broods with warm breast and with ah! bright wings.[2]

This poem was written in 1877 at the height of the Industrial Revolution. Hopkins knew about 'man's smudge...and people smeared with toil'. He ministered to the poor in Liverpool. He touched the deepest depths of depression in his final years in Dublin, writing what have come to be known as the 'Terrible Sonnets', and yet his final words were 'Oh, I am so happy!'

When we hear of Christ talking of 'glory' as he does in John 17, let that be the true note of glory. 'Father the hour has come; glorify your Son so that the Son may glorify you, since you have given him authority over all people, to give eternal life to all whom you have given him. And this is eternal life, that they may know you, the only true God and Jesus Christ whom you have sent. I glorified you on earth, by finishing the work that you gave me to do. So now, Father, glorify me in your presence with the glory that I had in your presence before the world existed' (Jn. 17.1–5).

We are attracted to the glory that lies in the natural world and nature is a sign of the even greater glory of God the Creator. But let us not stray too far from the glory that is the subject of this gospel. The Son is to be glorified. He is to be glorified through giving himself in death so that all may come to believe. It is to be a sacrificial glory. We hear it as a prayer. It is indeed a 'consecration' prayer.

John writes of Jesus, 'Jesus looked up to heaven and said, "Father, the hour has come"' (17.1). It is at this point that all our thoughts of creation are put aside for a while. Edwin Hoskyns writes, 'The prayer is a solemn consecration of himself in the presence of his disciples as their effective sacrifice; it is his prayer for glorification in and through his death; it is his irrevocable dedication of his disciples to their mission in the world, and his prayer that both they and those who believe through their teaching may be consecrated to the service of God; and finally, it concludes with the prayer that the Church thus consecrated may at the end behold the glory of the Son and dwell in the perfect love of the Father and the Son.'[3] Then the crucifixion will be complete and we can sing with Hopkins, 'the morning at the brown brink-eastward springs . . . with ah! bright wings.'

Glory is the result of consecration. Jesus consecrated himself to the work of the Father for our sakes. That work was a particular dying, which we imitate in our attempts at humility and in the receiving of the sacrament, for which this prayer in John 17 became a preparation in early liturgies. Jesus knows that the only glory worth having is the glory that comes from God. He and none other gives the glory. He and none other receives it back.

The light and the half-light

If we could gather all the four evangelists together into one room and ask them to share their memories and opinions of Jesus, we should listen in on a remarkable discussion. John would sit very quietly while Matthew, Mark and Luke shared their memories of some short epigrammatic sayings of Jesus and his semi-poetic aphorisms. In among those, in the way of the rabbis, they would throw out a parable or two and we should be delighted because they would be the stories we well remember ourselves. Three evangelists, exhausted with the excitement of their remembering, would eventually quieten down and look to John, wondering why he had been so silent; that perhaps they had been too excited and casual and gossipy, fearful of rebuke from the silent, wise one.

With John's first word the other evangelists would know they were not being rebuked. It was just that at last John had to come down to earth from having been temporarily in another world, another place. And so he would begin with a lengthy discourse, with its highly distinctive spiral form of argument, which set out from a grand statement. Then he would comment on that, winding round and round and enlarging on it and all the time preserving an admirable sequence. It is a tour de force, and he manages to include in this spiral argumentation the great miracles of the raising of Lazarus and the healing of the man born blind.

We read John's gospel and sense the authority of Jesus. Jesus moves towards the crucifixion with such stature and command. He reminds us of the dignity of our believing. We stand tall in our faith as we are about to inherit the kingdom formed for us from the beginning of time. We sense our unworthiness, but we need have no worries. If God is on our side who is against us? 'I did not lose a single one of those whom you gave me' (Jn. 18.9). This is strange because the first thing we hear in the lead-up to the crucifixion is of Judas betraying Jesus. Judas brought a detachment of soldiers together with police from the chief priests and the Pharisees, but we hear no more of him through John. Judas had played his part. He had received the dipped bread, 'and Satan had entered into him, and he went out and it was night' (Jn. 13.30). It was night indeed for him. He would have no more part in the light of Christ. He worked now only by the half-light of the soldiers' lanterns who came with weapons to the garden where Jesus was arrested. Judas had handed Jesus over.

Meanwhile, Jesus 'knew all that was to happen to him' (Jn. 18.4), that wonderful sense of knowledge bringing a calm assurance. This is the Son of the Father who created the world by his word. Jesus was the word that God spoke, all knowing, all reason. He stepped forward and asked the soldiers and the police, 'For whom are you looking?' (Jn. 18.4). The one who knows all things asks to know. He asks not to know for himself. *He* knows, but he asks so that those who reply may begin to know the full extent of what they do not yet know completely. They know enough to cause them to 'step back and fall to the ground' (18.6). Then Jesus asks them for the statutory third time, 'For whom are you looking?' (18.7). They say 'Jesus of Nazareth' which prompts Jesus to release the disciples from danger.

Simon Peter is an important figure among the disciples. He is a leader of people. John is the spiritual leader. John leans on the breast of Jesus at the Last Supper, closest to Jesus' heart. Simon Peter is a person of action 'who had a sword, drew it, struck the High Priest's slave, and cut off his right ear' (18.10). Jesus is again magisterial with Peter, 'Put up thy sword into the sheath' (Jn. 18.11)[4]. Is there an echo of those words in Shakespeare's 'Keep up your bright swords for the dew will rust them?'[5]

Yet Jesus is less concerned with the sword than with the cup of suffering, an echo of the Last Supper, which great event John does not describe. For John the sacrament of the blood is the cross itself where blood and water flow from the side of Christ to refresh the whole world. Jesus was bound (18.12) and led away to the religious court.

How delicately light fights with darkness in this part of the trial. Gerrit von Honhorst, the seventeenth-century artist, painted a picture that is well known and hangs in the National Gallery in London. A candle lights the scene from its central place on the table. Seated on the left of the table is Annas. He has one elbow on the table with a forefinger on a level with his eye, which looks up and directly at the eye of Jesus who stands at the right hand side of the table, hands bound. There are shady figures in the background. The book of the law is open in front of Annas. We witness, with the help of the artist, a moment in time held for eternity.

John, the writer, does what no painter can easily do. He presents us with two interweaved confrontations: one between Annas and Jesus and the other between Simon Peter and the High Priest's domestic staff. Peter was in denial, refusing to acknowledge his discipleship of Jesus. Jesus at his religious trial was responding to questions about his teaching with the subtlest of answers: 'If you want to know about the teacher, ask the ones he teaches' says Jesus. This gets him a blow on the face; and Jesus' verbal reply is a blow to their conscience. He asks them to answer their own question: 'If I have spoken wrongly, testify to the wrong. But if I have spoken rightly, why do you strike me?' (Jn. 18.23). Jesus is always returning the questions to strike at their hearts, their consciences and their law book.

We go back to Simon Peter. Jesus had maintained a silent witness to the truth. Peter denied all knowledge of the Lord and by his denial played false. 'At that moment the cock crowed' (Jn. 18.27) announcing a new day, the return of the light and the day of crucifixion.

My kingdom is not of this world

'They took Jesus from Caiaphas to Pilate's headquarters. It was early in the morning' (Jn. 18.28). John keeps us informed of the time and the weather. It was early. It was late. The cock crowed. He also keeps us abreast of the movements of Jesus over these few precious hours of Christian memory. Jesus was moved from pillar to post, from the religious headquarters of the High Priest to the headquarters of the secular powers, the seat of Pontius Pilate, governor of Judea. Pilate was the emperor's representative who was concerned with keeping the peace and collecting taxes, and was responsible for the unenviable task of releasing one popular prisoner during Passover. Worldly stuff if ever there was.

Into this pragmatic, routine, small-country politics, were dropped the most remarkable and explosive words of Jesus that have reverberated through time ever since. Pilate: 'I am not a Jew, am I? Your own nation and the chief priests have handed you over to me. What have you done?' Jesus: 'My kingdom is not from this world' (Jn. 18.35–36).

This is not a popular text in the modern Church, rarely preached on. It challenges all our preconceptions of mission and ministry. It focuses on what Jesus actually meant by this revolutionary statement. He clarifies it a little. If Pilate believed that Jesus was trying to take over the state and organize a coup, then he need not have worried. Nothing could have been further from Jesus' mind, although he attracted followers who would have welcomed that at least as part of his agenda. 'But as it is' said Jesus, 'my kingdom is not from here' (Jn. 18.36).

Christ's kingdom was then and is still an idea of God; not a place but a person. Kingship, headship, power and ultimately truth are invested in God and God is known to us as the creator and sustainer of being and the miracle is that God at this particular moment of history, the moment of crucifixion, becomes known to us in Jesus Christ. We look at Christ and we imagine God and they are the same. 'The Word became flesh and lived among us . . . full of grace and truth' (Jn. 1.14). 'He came to what was his own and his own people did not accept him. But to all who received him, who believed in his name, he gave power to become children of God, who were *born*, not of blood or of the will of the flesh or of the will of man, but of God' (Jn. 1.11–13).

Faith takes us into the mystery. Those who have entered into that mystery will know its glories and its tribulations. The cross points both upwards and downwards and this world is our cross. 'In the world you will face persecution,' said Jesus, 'but take courage, I have conquered the world' (Jn. 16.33). But we rush ahead. It is time to pause over Pilate's classic question, 'What is truth?' and to ponder Jesus' response to it. Jesus tells Pilate that his main purpose was not to cause conflict. He was not an insurgent. He had no desire to wage war, or commit an act of violence; these were all acts which Pilate would have had a responsibility to quash and punish.

Jesus says that his purpose is *to testify*, in Greek, 'to be a martyr to the truth'. Truth for Jesus was not so much something that you told, but that you belonged to. Jesus saw it as an indwelling in the embodied truth of God, a making your home in the mansion of God's nature. Pilate asks Jesus, 'What is truth?' (Jn. 18.38). Pilate is not concerned with absolute truth; he is concerned with the truth of the matter in hand. 'There is nothing of real reverence or seriousness in Pilate's words, still less of awe. He does not shape, even in passing thought, a subject for earnest enquiry, but half sadly, half cynically, implies that even in ordinary matters truth is unattainable. It was so evidently on his mind in the matter before him, but so much at least was plain to his Roman clearness of vision, that the prisoner accused by his countrymen was no political intriguer. Pilate therefore impatiently breaks off the examination which had (as he fancied) shown enough to decide the case that he may obtain the release of Jesus if possible.'[6]

So the administrative machinery of this tin-pot regime clanked on. Pilate went out again to the people and this time, dangerously, he gave them a choice. The Passover privilege of the freeing of one of the prisoners through acclaim of the crowd meant that Barabbas was freed and Jesus was condemned to death. Barabbas 'was one of those outlaws who not infrequently cover their violence with a cloak of patriotism. The pathos of that final sentence is so typical of John the evangelist.'[7] It indicates so much more than it says. 'Now Barabbas was a bandit' (Jn. 18.40).

'He goes his way to the Father'

There was both a physical and a mental battle going on at the crucifixion. The accounts of the crucifixion do not dwell on the horror or the pain. Since then, artists, writers and film-makers have dwelt on it, but the evangelists did not. Certainly they record enough of it to make us feel the physical suffering: 'Pilate took Jesus and had him flogged. And the soldiers wove a crown of thorns and put it on his head ... they kept coming up to him, saying, "Hail! King of the Jews!", and striking him on the face' (Jn. 19.3). The crowds taunted him. He carried the cross. He felt a desperate thirst.

Yet, the evangelists were not concerned to shock us with the extremes of torture, for they had another purpose in their writing and that was to do with 'who Jesus was'. This does not involve the crowds; they love a hunt and a kill. The gospel was not written to impress the voyeur within us, but, more importantly, to evoke faith in God. The gospels have an altogether different purpose to the blockbuster movie. The gospels fix our gaze on Christ and compel us to choose our priority: the world's prizes, or the crucified Christ?

We fix our gaze on Christ and what do we see? We see someone who is the still centre of the turning world. We recall him doing his theology, his praying and thinking in the street, in the courtroom, in the small upper rooms of Jerusalem, on his knees on the hillside, beside the olive trees. Above all and paradoxically we hear his theology in the silence and in the few words that break that silence on the cross. These few words tell us the truth about God, about himself and about us. The truth about God is that God cares. The truth about Christ is that he loved and to love he had to suffer. But why? Why did he have to suffer? Why did the one who made the universe in all its majesty and intricacy, gave us life and breath and the ability to think and to choose to love or not, have to reveal his true nature to us on the cross? Were there not better ways? Why did he hide in a paradox to which no one at the time could find an answer? I expect we would have been as perplexed as everybody else.

The cross is absurd. It breaks all the rules. God on a cross, naked, thirsty, the maker of all things powerless to unmake this. Why do we persist against all the odds? We care for at least two reasons that I can think of. One is to honour the source of our faith. God touches us with his story, through the teachers and preachers and, yes, through the films too and the plays and the pictures. And that touch that unforgettable touch opens us up to the world of faith and trust in the reality of God, though unseen. We follow each Easter to the foot of the cross because we glimpse there the source of love. Once more we focus on the one good person remaining true to God for our sakes. That moves our hearts, it moves our humanity, it moves our deep sense of what is true and, as Dante would say, it moves the sun and the stars and the entire universe as well.

The cross also challenges us to place our faith in Christ in front of the world, to go public in whatever way we are called to, as Christ went public in the highways and byways of Galilee and Judea. To go public and put our talents out in the sun to grow, or so that Christ can work through us in the skill of the Holy Spirit, as healers, teachers, or as contemplatives praying on behalf of others.

'So they took Jesus, and carrying the cross by himself, he went out to what is called The Place of the Skull, which in Hebrew is Golgotha. There they crucified him, and with him two others, one on either side, with Jesus between them' (Jn. 19.16–18). We began at the beginning and now we end. And there are some telling final images to take with us. Jesus, as he is handing himself over to his heavenly Father, hands his human mother, Mary, into the care of John: a final act which takes us right back to the beginning of Jesus' human life, the day the Word became flesh and began to live among us.

Then began the distribution of the only worldly goods he seemed to have left, his clothes and his tunic. His clothes they divided, his tunic was seamless, woven in one piece from the top. This they cast lots for, fulfilling the prediction of Psalm 22.18, 'They divide my garments among them; they cast lots for my clothing.' And finally, Jesus said, 'I am thirsty' (Jn. 19.28), to fulfil the prediction of Psalm 69 'and when I was thirsty they gave me vinegar to drink.' 'Then he bowed his head and gave up his spirit' (Jn. 19.30). 'His final act is to give up – of course to the Father – that spirit which was always close to the Father's heart. He goes his way to the Father.'[8]

The resurrection: In the beginning again

One of the strongest, though what might be considered one of the weakest, features of the resurrection is the gentleness with which Christ returns. We might think the resurrection would have deserved more of a flourish, trumpets and a brass band at least, but Christ returns with peace, assurance, comfort and at least three times he appears in the context of food, at Emmaus, in the Upper Room, and beside Lake Galilee. It is this peacefulness that is so persuasive. Christ makes every attempt to remove fear and replace it with faith. The resurrection is a time for reassurance and strengthening in the faith.

We are unlikely ever to know for certain in a scientific or historical sense about the exact details of the resurrection and certainly not in a way that would satisfy a court of law, although the debate is bound to continue. There seem to be at least three reasons why it would be reasonable to believe that Jesus did rise from the dead. The scriptural evidence continues to plead a naïve authority. The accounts are written in a tone and voice in which it would seem impossible deliberately to mislead. Also, Christ has remained a central figure for millions of people since the first Easter Sunday and the reality that he is alive in people's hearts and minds is plainly evident. Something must have provided the first stimulus, something strong enough to maintain this unending momentum. The appearance of Christ alive after his death is the origin of that momentum.

Thirdly, no one had anything material to gain from making the story up. The writers would gain no status, no wealth and no intellectual credibility. On the contrary, they laid themselves open to persecution, ribaldry, prison and martyrdom. The Acts of the Apostles and the letters of Paul written from prison bear witness to the circumstances in which the resurrection was proclaimed, and they were not propitious. In addition to these thoughts lies one that is nothing to do with evidence – more with a sense of rightness and truth in its wider context.

The greeting with which Christ returned from the dead was 'Peace be with you!' There was nothing ghoulish or over-dramatic about his return. He came to calm, to allay fears, not to excite. The atmosphere in which Jesus had his encounters with others is subsumed in a sense of awe and tranquillity. The brief statements breathe confidence and a gentle authority. They even overlap and apparently conflict: 'Do not hold on to me,' (Jn. 20.17) says Jesus to Mary Magdalene, and 'Put your finger here' (Jn. 20.27) to Thomas. He came to strengthen faith and reduce fear and for each he seemed to have a personal message.

Christ's earthly task was done. Now it was the disciples' turn to proclaim the gospel. Christ came to them to strengthen their faith and to remove their fear. The less the fear, the stronger the faith. Christ was all faith. To see the resurrected Christ was to see what faith really looked like. In Christ was a picture of a complete trust in God. As we live in Christ, as we learn and pray to live in Christ, we too will experience a deeper and deeper faith, with less and less fear, for we shall come to know that in Christ we have the security of eternal life.

It was the resurrection that initiated the writing of the story, not the story that drove the resurrection. It was in the strength of the resurrection that the evangelists traced their story of faith and doubt. Paul, the last of the apostles, rather than writing the story of the struggle of faith and doubt in the earthly ministry of Jesus, wrote out of a personal experience of sharing in the resurrection glory. Everything he wrote was from within a dramatic experience of faith. In Christ he had found a way to the understanding of the nature of God, who was a cause for praise and became the inspiration to foster and encourage the Church on earth. The explosion of creativity within Paul was generated by his finding a mystery solved by love. He was seemingly uninterested in the facts of Christ's life, except his triumph over death and the resurrection to eternal life. That mystery solved by love is something we can be part of through faith.

The New Testament was inspired by the resurrection of Jesus Christ. It was at that point that literature was uniquely put at the disposal of faith. We treasure its heritage in the Old Testament, for those roots go very deep and feed the New Testament. At points they are inextricable, but the real driving force of the New Testament is the raising of Christ from the dead, defeating the old enemy, death, and opening out hope to all who have faith in the power of Christ Jesus to save.

The Christian journey is never an individual one. However solitary we may sometimes feel or even desire to be, we belong to Christ's body on earth, the Church, through our baptism. It is our responsibility, inspired by our faith in God, to maintain the memory of Christ and his resurrection. Memories can become like museums. Museums are useful and can be very inspiring places, but the Church is not a museum and needs constantly to be refreshed by the presence of the risen Christ among us. We say in the Eucharist: 'The Lord is here,' and the response comes back, 'His Spirit is with us.'

He is with us to inspire us. He gives us the strength to love the people *he* loved back into health and wholeness of living, and into peace. We continue with his priorities for the marginalized, the bullied and those manipulated or enslaved for what they can give and not for what they might wish to receive. The ascended Christ has not gone upwards for safety, but as a means of being a universal presence through the Holy Spirit, to bring judgement to bear on the wickedness of human nature and to be a friend of the vulnerable. He offers his love to all, but he refuses to force it beyond a person's desire to receive it. The Church should have a desire to be the place where Christ's mind prevails. We need to wait on that mind which, translated by prayer, can then be shared with those thirsty for the refreshment only Christ can bring.

Notes

1   Friedrich von Hügel, *Selected Writings* (London: Fontana Books, 1964), pp. 101, 2.
2   'God's Grandeur', lines 10–14, in *The Poetical Works of Gerard Manley Hopkins*, Norman H. Mackenzie (ed.) (Oxford: Oxford University Press, 1990), p. 139.
3   Edwyn Clement Hoskyns, *The Fourth Gospel, Volume Two* (London: Faber, 1940), p. 586.
4   John 18.11 quoted from the Authorized Version.
5   W. Shakespeare, *Othello* 1.2.59.
6   B.F. Westcott, *The Gospel According to St John* (London: John Murray, 1882; seventeenth impression, 1924), p. 261.
7   Ibid., p. 262.
8   William Temple, *Readings in St John's Gospel* (London: Macmillan, 1947), p. 369.